The Philosophy of the I Ching

The Philosophy

of the

I Ching

Carol K. Anthony

Anthony Publishing Company
Stow, Massachusetts 01775

Anthony Publishing Company
218 Gleasondale Road, Stow, Massachusetts 01775

Library of Congress Card Number 81-69537
ISBN-0-9603832-1-2

Printed in the United States of America
Cover design by Jeanne Seronde

Contents

Contents

Preface

The title of this book was chosen as the best explanation of its contents. The everyday bookstore browser will pick up this book because it contains an explanation of the *I Ching* way. But, in the larger meaning of *philosophy,* there is no such thing as a philosophy of the *I Ching.* It is no system of belief, nor is it a systematized explanation of our existence. The philosophical explanation given in Book II of the *I Ching* was written a thousand years after the oldest part—Book I—originated, in an attempt to explain its cosmological basis. This explanation avoids making a philosophical statement. Similarly, I have not attempted to give a complete philosophical system, as philosophers do, but have tried to indicate the way of the *I Ching* as it helps us solve problems, and as it guides us to an understanding of the higher life of the spirit.

Using the *I Ching* as a daily guide leads us through a process of self-development that satisfies our innate search for the meaning of existence. Our understanding does not come by way of intellectual study, but through experiences that cause us to penetrate the deepest reaches of our intuitive awareness. In time, we learn to depend upon that awareness as the most appropriate basis for action. Cultivating and depending upon that awareness is the way of the *I Ching.*

This book is based on a series of six lectures given in Stow and Lexington, Massachusetts, in 1980 and 1981. These lectures served as an overview—not a comprehensive, but a minimum overview. In this book I have elaborated on, and expanded, this highly condensed material.

In organizing this overview, I have devoted myself entirely to the message of the *I Ching* as it has communicated itself to me. I have avoided inserting into it any *a priori* belief system by comparing it to my own protestent Christian background. In the same way I have avoided incorporating into it other philosophical systems which are similar. Rather, I have tried to be a servant and adherent, than a commentator on the *I Ching*. Where it has led, I have followed. If, in doing so I have helped others in their study of the *I Ching*, I will be well satisfied.

This book does not attempt to serve the same purpose as *A Guide to the I Ching*, my first book on this subject, which is more a manual of interpretation. However, the reader will find that this book further clarifies the "Guide," and the "Guide" similarly helps clarify this book. They are complementary in nature.

As in all such undertakings we are dependent upon the good services of many people who come forward to help—one with an insight here, another with a vital omission there. To them I render my sincere thanks and appreciation. As for those who have committed themselves to the heavy services of manuscript preparation, I am particularly endebted to Nancy Hamilton, Faith Regamey, Sarah Wilder, and Karen Anthony. I also wish to thank Jeanne Seronde for providing the cover design which I feel so well suits our work.

Introduction

In a meditation experience I saw many bowls of different salads ranged before me on a sideboard. At the right end was the salad of the master chef. It was the ultimate salad prepared by the great Sage who speaks through the *I Ching*. The other bowls were salads prepared by other chefs. All were good edible salads. Then I saw the eclectic person going along the row of salads, picking an olive from the top of one, carrot strips from the top of another, and bits and pieces of this and that, making up his own salad. This was a perfectly acceptable salad, but it was not the same salad as that of the master chef. The eclectic is trying, in taking bits and pieces, to approximate the salad of the master chef, but he cannot succeed because he knows only some of the ingredients—only those he sees on top—and he does not know the proportions that create the final balance.

Then I saw my mother's fruitcake. Everyone raved about it and wanted the recipe, but on discovering how expensive the ingredients were, they began to substitute cheaper ones. The fruitcakes they made were good, but they were not the same fruitcake everyone so admired.

The value of eclecticism is that of bringing one to the sideboard in the first place. We all wish to sample the different foods offered. But if one wishes to understand a particular way of life, it is necessary to put that recipe together and not merely sample it, but eat it. In no other way can one receive its great nourishment, or know its true value. If a reader wants to understand the way of the *I Ching,* he will progress more readily if he avoids maintaining an elevated, critical view, as if he were trying to see all the ingredients from a purely external, intellectual vantage point. By limiting himself to his intellect, he will only see the surface and never experience the depths. He will never fully realize the proportions, the inner balance, the wonderful nourishment and fulfillment of this great-tasting mixture, but will remain isolated by his mistrust, his fear, and his desire to be the master. To be led by a great master, such as the *I Ching,* we must truly be led. To be taught by a great teacher, we must truly open our minds and be receptive, otherwise the *I Ching* will remain elusive and mysterious.

By consulting the *I Ching* we obtain a reflection of what we intuitively know. The *I Ching* "reply" confirms and reinforces this knowledge so that, in whatever areas of our perception we have lost our way, we may re-learn how to be true to ourselves. The *I Ching,* in this respect is occult. That a mere book can act in a teaching capacity through being consulted puts it in the category of the mysterious, because no one can say how it works. That it does work is a fact that millions of Asians have observed for thousands of years.

What we learn through the *I Ching* is a substratum of universal truth that underlies all major religions and philosophies of life. As these universal truths emerge in our learning, we understand the relationships that these truths have to philosophies and religions. By contrast to them, however, the *I Ching* way is to live in an unstructured manner, free of precepts and rules. Just as we constantly interact with the changing environment as we canoe down a river, so we learn, through the *I Ching,* to interact with our continuously changing lives. With the *I Ching* as guide, we learn our natural limitations; as we apply our knowledge, we gain experience; we avoid rocks and underwater objects; we find the channel; we learn when to paddle hard and when to rest, when to get out of the water and portage around dangerous falls. We start with the stream when it is small, at a time when our errors are less serious; then, down river, we are able to face the larger challenges. We are never totally secure; we can never plot what we are going to do more than a few feet ahead. This means we continuously adapt to the conditions as they show themselves. In finding that our abilities are up to the challenges, we develop the courage to take the risks that are always involved in a continuous learning process. Although we have a master guide in the Sage who speaks through the *I Ching,* who knows what lies ahead, throughout the trip we are only helped to develop our skills. It is we who make the trip, who do the paddling, who take the risks, and who, in the end, become our own masters.

The way of the *I Ching,* inasmuch as those who follow it find themselves in spiritual agreement, would appear to be a philosophy. Because they are aware of their limitations, it would appear to others that they proceed by rules. Because, through their experience they are aware of the channeling embankments and obstructions, it would appear that they are bound by precepts. All these appearances, however, are illusions. They have all travelled the same river. At the beginning of their voyage they had no fear; through encountering the risks and dangers, they became aware of their fear; gradually, because they developed their skills and learned to trust their guide, they became free of their fear. Together, they laugh at the fears they have overcome; they understand each other without much ado and feel a community of spirit. What they have learned of the river is the extent of their philosophy, which, at any moment, might be enlarged by a new insight.

I.

The I Ching, *An Overview*

Its Historic Significance

Although it is not the oldest Chinese document, the *I Ching or Book of Changes* was formed in such antiquity that, in the words of Iulian Shchutskii, one of the foremost Western sinologists, "no other classical book can compete with it in chronological priority." The *I Ching* is estimated to be at least five thousand years old and thought to be the work of a legendary ruler of antiquity, Fu Shi. Revised thirty-one hundred years ago by King Wen and his son, the Duke of Chou (founders of the Chou Dynasty of China), it was edited and annotated by Confucious six hundred years later. Due to the reverence paid it by that great sage, the *I Ching* is considered to be the most important Confucian classic text.

For centuries the classic Confucian texts were the basis of formal education, not only in China but also in Japan, Korea, Vietnam, and other countries which adopted the Chinese culture. Of these texts, Shchutskii stated that their influence "in philosophy, in mathematics, in politics, in strategy, in the theory of painting and music, and in art..." was fundamental, and so grounded in the *I Ching* that it is impossible to understand them without first undertaking a study of the *I Ching* itself. I asked a contemporary Chinese businessman about the significance of the *I Ching* in today's Chinese culture; without hesitation he replied that "The Chinese culture *is* the *I Ching*," explaining that it is so incorporated into the culture that there is no other way to describe its influence; until very recently, every educated person had to memorize it. Both he and Japanese businessmen I met, have confirmed that there is an *I Ching* scholar, or "Sage," in nearly every Chinese and Japanese community, to whom people may turn for help in its interpretation, and for consultation on important matters.

1

The *I Ching* was associated with Confucianism—the religion of China's ruling class for many centuries—with Taoism, and indirectly with Zen Buddhism. Lao Tzu's book the *Tao Teh Ching,* became the foundation of the Taoist philosophy, the fundamental concepts of which are implicit in the *I Ching.* The *I Ching* explains the *Tao Teh Ching* as the *Tao Teh Ching* explains the *I Ching.* A student of the *Tao Teh Ching,* Chuang Tzu, was one of the founders of Zen Buddhism. It is said that Buddhism went to China and became Chinese. Many of the concepts of the *I Ching* were incorporated into Zen Buddhism. It is undoubtedly for such reasons that Shchutskii remarked, "We may call it the first book in the Chinese library."

The importance of the *I Ching* has continued from that day to this. Up until the beginning of the 20th Century the *I Ching* remained a mystery in the Western world. Some 19th Century translations were made, but while these translators were competent in the language, they were unacquainted with the philosophy of the *I Ching,* and failed to understand the reasons for its importance. Richard Wilhelm, a Christian missionary, was the first to study it from the "standpoint of the Chinese themselves." He was guided by a "scholar of the old school, one of the last of his kind, who knew thoroughly the great field of commentary literature that had grown up around the book in the course of the ages." Wilhelm's translation appeared in 1924, and made it possible for Westerners to use the book as it is used throughout the East. (This translation became available in English in 1950.) While the importance of the *I Ching* on a world-wide basis is still in its beginnings, it has already met with great favor. The expansion of its influence is undoubtedly due to Wilhelm's work, and to the great stimulus given it by Carl G. Jung and the Jungian school of psychoanalysis.

The *I*

The word *ching* simply means classic text and is appended to the titles of all classic Chinese texts, e.g. *Tao Teh Ching* and *Shu Ching.* The complete title, therefore, is *I,* or *Chou I,* as the *I Ching* is sometimes called, because King Wen of the Chou Dynasty compiled and enlarged existing materials into

2

the current book, which he then called *I*. In its original meaning and subsequent connotations, *I* synthesizes the book's essential philosophical contents.

The original meaning of *I*, according to Wilhelm, was *lizard*, but in particular the chameleon, symbolizing changeability and easy mobility; it also contains the concept of what happens easily, without effort. This meaning was merged with another, visually similar character, which meant command—the banner of a commander, or a command granted a vassal by his feudal lord as a reward for faithful service. Thus *I* has the implication of power and the transferring of power. Since a command given by one higher to one lower also stood for the fixed relationship between what is above and what is below, *I* implies constancy in relating correctly, the higher being dependable (a person one can count on), the lower faithfully serving, and following, or being led. The word also contained the idea of the sun and moon, representing the Yang and Yin, the two fundamental forces of change, and the immutable law governing change called the *Tao*. All these implications were summed up by an early commentary Wilhelm quotes: "The name *I* has three meanings: These are the easy, the changing, and the constant." This means: what we see with clarity is easy to accomplish. The whole purpose of consulting the *I Ching* is to attain the clarity of mind which leads to constancy of character. Constancy, in turn, develops one's power of command in the service of that which is higher than one's self—a service which fulfills our life's purpose.

Wilhelm describes 'the easy' as an uncomplicated simplicity of mind which is the starting point for understanding and attaining clarity. "We miss the meaning of this system if at the outset we look for something dark and mysterious in it." He adds, "The situations depicted in the *Book of Changes* are the primary data of life—what happens to everybody every day, and what is simple and easy to understand." Thus, the simple and the easy that Wilhelm calls the "gateway" to understanding the *Book of Changes* correspond to the humility of an unstructured, open mind.

Wilhelm describes 'the changing' as an externally dynamic process through which man may develop his perspective and realize the meaning of life. To resist movement, to barricade ourselves against the natural flow, is to miss the opportunity for growth and development into a higher being. "To stand in the stream of this development is a datum of nature; to recognize it and follow it is responsibility and free choice."

The third element, 'the constant', also implies the secure, as in security from danger and the unknown, and from misfortune. "Safety is the clear knowledge of the right stand to be taken, security in the assurance that events are unrolling in the right direction." Such security comes from the human virtue of reliability. Indeed, in the *I Ching* there is no greater power or security than that contained in constancy—the power of enduring in harmony with the Cosmic Laws.

While the word *I* symbolizes the natural law of change, *I* also implies the means of adapting to change through simplicity and constancy; it further refers to the power for good that accrues to the person who learns its secrets and follows its way.

The Books Which Comprise the *I Ching*

The *I Ching* is composed of three books. Book I, with its 64 sections, is the original *Chou I,* or divinatory manual. These 64 sections are based on 64 different six-lined figures called hexagrams. With their accompanying explanations, the hexagrams comprise the working part of the book, which is consulted by means of chance. Each of the hexagrams describes a different specific circumstance or state of mind, and gives counsel for relating correctly to that circumstance.

The methods of consulting it vary, but chance is the means employed. Coins may be tossed, or yarrow stalks dropped. In either case, six number combinations are obtained which indicate either yang or yin lines. Once the lines are drawn into a hexagram, it is looked up in the *I Ching* and read.

Book II, a collection of commentaries, thought by Wilhelm to be of the Confucian school, "intended to disclose the material out of which that world of ideas [expressed in Book I] arose." This book synthesizes the view of the cosmos implied in Book I and its philosophy.

Book III is a sort of glossary. Shchutskii says, "They are rather a collection of quotations from various authors, whose names were not preserved," and they are "commentaries, not

4

the basic text." Like Book II, Book III was added to the original text.

The Traditional Use of the *I Ching*

From their beginning, the 64 hexagrams have served as a language through which the user can consult the Higher Power, the Unknown, or, as the *I Ching* calls it, the great Sage. In Book II of the *I Ching* it is said that the ancient sages, through meditation, assigned meanings to the hexagrams and their appended lines in such a way that all possible situations could be reflected. In their totality, the hexagrams range in varying gradations from "all positive" to "all negative." In consulting the Sage by means of chance, one of the 64 hexagrams was pointed to as communicating the Sage's message. Chance was deemed to be a particularly suitable method since no prior meaning could be implied in chance; it was a way of placing the selection of the reading in the hands of the Unknown.

The *I Ching* has been consulted to resolve questions of doubt in exactly the same way we flip a coin to decide something. Because we cannot decide we say, "Let Fate decide." In the West we usually resolve only unimportant matters in this way, such as who goes first in a ball game. In the East, however, it is believed that in important matters one must consult the Higher Power, which alone knows the hidden elements which make the difference between success and failure. This is because, in the Eastern way of thinking, life is a smaller, inferior system within a larger, superior system that is hidden from our view. The ant walking across the floor is unaware of the fate that may await it beneath our feet; similarly, we are unaware of the larger sphere of action that affects our activities. To avoid calamity, Easterners have consulted the Unknown for guidance past the unseen dangers.

Not every question is put to the *I Ching*. For the ordinary affairs and the ordinary times of life our experience and intellectual capabilities are considered to be sufficient. In questions of doubt or in extraordinary times, however, the *I Ching*, in the hexagram called *Grace* (22), says that it is necessary to be more earnest and to find help. This refers to the help the *I Ching* can give. Through consulting it, we are

5

given counsel that enables us to minimize, or negate, potentially harmful circumstances.

In all questions of doubt, we experience a moment of inner conflict, or hesitation. This happens because intuitively we already know the answer, but our intellect, with its considerations, overshadows and overpowers this knowledge. Intuitive knowledge contains a cosmic logic that the intellect cannot perceive, yet when our intellect is made aware of this logic, it agrees as if to say, "Why didn't I see that? It's so simple." The intellect does not have access to cosmic logic because intuitive knowledge is undifferentiated and unconscious, unlike the differentiated sciences of chemistry, physics, and biology, which belong to the realm of the intellect.

The hexagrams we receive in the daily consultation concern the way we have related to the day's circumstances, or how we will need to adapt to up-coming events if we are to meet them correctly. The adaptation required usually consists of changing a narrow, subjective attitude to one more detached and universal, which is in harmony with the universe. Through this experiential way of being taught, our learning rests not on precept and rule, but on what the *I Ching* calls inner truth. What we learn in the mind is that day verified by experience, and the relationship between the external reality and the hidden world that governs it, is directly perceived. This process yields an awareness that becomes what Eastern philosophies call a state of enlightenment. The *I Ching,* however, simply calls such a person "the superior man."

The Sage

Several hexagrams define the Unknown to whom we speak when we consult the *I Ching*. The fourth hexagram, *Youthful Folly* (4), defines this Unknown as a sage who is capable of teaching us the workings of the inner world. It is we who must seek the Sage, not the Sage who seeks us. If we are to learn, we must be open-minded. The *I Ching* also calls itself a well with clear, refreshing water which is available to all who come. The well also symbolizes our self in our intuitive awareness, in our inmost reaches of consciousness, and in our unconscious mind. In order to draw water from the well we must put down our rope. This symbolizes sincerity in seeking, for, if we have an indifferent or doubtful attitude, we have a "cracked jug" that will not hold water. If we seek only to find support for inferior ideas, we drink "the mud of the well." If we seek help to further selfish aims, we only "catch fishes." When it is not time to know the answers or to achieve our goals, we are told, "the well is being lined." The water of the well is symbolic not only of truth but of the universality of truth that lies like a water-table under all the wells of a community. This universal truth exists in everyone in the form of their intuitive and unconscious knowledge. It is a sort of lowest common denominator which applies equally to everyone. If an idea about human behavior is not universally applicable, for instance, it is not truth. Also, truth is always refreshing and light. If we think "that can't be truth, it's too grim (or dark)," it isn't—our perception is still incomplete. Truth is always refreshing and good, lifting off the burdens of doubt and fear. Both great and small perceptions have this quality.

The Sage who speaks through the *I Ching* defines himself in other hexagrams as "an expert in directing affairs," "a man of influence who has special abilities," "a guest who knows the secrets by which the kingdom may be made to flourish," "a ruler," "a prince who seeks able helpers," and a helpful friend in many other lines. The Sage is also referred to in the plural in some lines, such as in the following, as "persons in retirement who may be sought for help in difficult matters if we approach them modestly."

In consulting the *I Ching* regularly, we see that a way of life emerges. This way begins with our first consultation. We put our first question to the Unknown through being open-minded enough to throw the coins; in so doing we demonstrate a sort of humility and accessibility to being guided. Humility and accessibility are attitudes which arouse and complete the power of the Creative. Once aroused, the Creative acts to 'further', or aid us. Having humility and being accessible is what the *I Ching* calls being receptive. Cultivating receptivity develops the habit of inner listening, which enables us to be led by our intuition.

Not that a slavish use of the *I Ching* is encouraged, but we may require a considerable time in working with it if we are to re-new our natural ability to listen within. In our culture, we are unaccustomed to listening to the voice of our intuition. We may have even lost our ability to know, from the intuitive viewpoint, what are important and what are unimportant questions. We find, in using the *I Ching,* however, that the Sage ignores superficial questions, and speaks only on the things of real concern. Furthermore, he stays on the same subject until we have understood the message.

I Ching Cosmology

Book II summarizes the concepts incorporated in Book I of the *I Ching.* The source of all things, it says, is called *T'ai Chi,* which means 'oneness' and 'primal unity'. This primal source is also called the Void, or Container of the Universe. It is seen as changeless, timeless, and universal, and as empty space. It "works" in ways analogous to the way the human mind works, and the implication is always there that the primal source of all things is the Cosmic Mind. In the human mind a thought arises in the empty space; this thought gives rise to action. In the Cosmic Mind, the image arises; it is called the Yang, or Creative Force; its presence arouses its opposite, the Yin, or Receptive Force, which meets it halfway. Through the nurturing action of Yin, the image is brought into being. These two forces, Yang and Yin, are the primary opposites; their interaction is seen to give rise to all things. In Western thought, opposites are said to annihilate each other, but in Eastern thought they are said to arouse and complete each other, creating the eternal wheel of change. In the human mind the creative image comes through the intuitive, yang faculty; this image is nurtured by the intellect and brought into existence. Intellect, in Eastern thought, is a yin faculty.

Everything comes into existence in this way—every thing, every happening, every sequence of happenings. Thus the Yang and Yin—the creative and receptive powers—are forces in cyclical motion, ever changing and creating new conditions. They are, with all this motion, set in the Void, which is motionless, timeless, eternal, and unchanging. Thus the Void, or T'ai Chi, comprises and determines all; it is the origin and ultimate container of all things in their totality. The structure of the atom seems to be the best analogy of the changing set within the unchanging. Electrons revolve around a nucleus of particles within an envelope of empty space. The empty space is integral to the structure of the atom, as T'ai Chi is integral to the structure of existence.

Of these two primal forces, Yang, which arises first as a determiner, is seen as superior to Yin, in the way that the seasons are seen as determiners of when to plant. Yang is first in order because it is germinal. All life contains the primal forces in microcosm. All things in existence are seen as demonstrating more or less of yang and yin principles, thus everything can be grouped in either yang or yin categories of opposites. The following list is an example of yang-yin categorizing:

Yang	Yin
Image	Reality
Heaven	Earth
Odd numbers	Even numbers
Masculine Principle	Feminine principle
Light	Darkness

Human beings contain both primal powers in microcosm. We have both superior and inferior natures. We have both masculine and feminine components in our natures. Through our intuition we have access to the inner, spiritual, hidden world of heaven; through our intellect we have access to the outer, material, evident world of earth and nature. The structure of the hexagram reflects these relationships. For example, a hexagram is composed of six lines. The three bottom lines are called the earth trigram and the three top lines, the heaven trigram. The hexagram is also seen in another way, with the bottom two lines representing earth, the middle two representing human beings, and the top two representing heaven. Consequently, it is said that human beings, represented by the middle two lines, have a line in both the heaven and earth trigrams. Having both these forces within us, we are seen as free to choose to follow either the way of heaven within—our superior nature—or the way of earth without—our inferior nature. However, the first hexagram, *The Creative,* explains that our ultimate destiny is to use this

9

lifetime to complete within ourselves, through self-development, the true and superior image of us stored in the mind of the Deity. Thus, this life, having its full array of opposites, is a place for experiencing and fulfilling the meaning of our existence through the fullest development of our natures. As our ultimate destiny, it is also called our personal Tao.

Tao

Tao is a word that has no suitable Western counterpart. It is pronounced both "dow" as in Dow-Jones, and "toe." The interaction of the two primal forces, Yang and Yin, is called the great Tao of the universe. Tao is also called the ridgepole of the universe, and the Unifying Principle. It is the ridgepole because it is firm—the immutable law which governs change. I see it most as the Cosmic Will. The Tao is at work in human beings in microcosm as human will. The ridgepole is seen as our will to follow what is great in ourselves—our original, true, superior natures—and to see the life process through to the end in conscious willingness and acceptance. The 28th hexagram, *Preponderance of the Great,* concerns the human ridgepole, or will to follow the good during times of stress. This hexagram could be subtitled "Great Stress Preponderates," because we tend to draw it during times of stress. At one point the ridgepole is seen to "sag to the breaking point." This happens because we depart from following what is good in ourselves through giving way to feelings of doubt and hopelessness. Another line refers to "bracing the ridgepole." Similarly, in *Darkening of the Light* (36), our will to follow the good and the beautiful is endangered by doubt and hopelessness; we are responding to the temptation to give up, or have already done so. *The Abysmal* (29) addresses the danger that occurs to our will when we put forth great effort to achieve visible progress, and fail. The great ridgepole of the universe, the great Tao, is seen as perfected will, free of doubt, firm in principle, immutable, always continuing the forces of regeneration, of life, of change, of light. It is a part of our personal Tao, or destiny, to mirror this great will unerringly; in doing so we achieve our life's highest purpose and fulfillment.

Tao is also called the Unifying Principle because it

shapes the disparate elements into meaningful things, bringing order out of chaos, harmony out of discordant elements, and unity out of divergent trends of action. As such, Tao is the Theme which underlies all seemingly unrelated events. If we look back at the photographs of a 25-year-old, we see in his infancy and youth, features of the adult; yet at no time can we have seen the adult characteristics in the child. There exists in these photographs a Theme which finds expression in the adult; this Theme is another word for Tao. Sometimes in finding the occupation that most fulfills us, we look back at seemingly unrelated things we did that fit extremely well into what we now do. At any point of our development we might have said, "My life is going nowhere!" But the Theme has run through it all, as when one tacks a boat along a line of wind; first the boat heads in one direction, then in another, but it always makes progress in one overall direction. Tao, the Unifying Principle, gives meaning to our lives. This Theme, however, is not predestination; rather, it is the unique capacity of Tao to give unity to everything we have done, once we observe and adapt to its immutable laws. Tao is like a carpenter: through the power of the Creative the different shapes and sizes of things are joined into the most appropriate forms. Everything we do is capable of being constructively used for higher purposes by the Tao. The second line of *The Receptive* (2) refers explicitly to this: "Straight, square, great, yet nothing remains unfurthered." The commentary speaks of lines that may be drawn into squares and squares that may be drawn into cubes; even small pieces of straight lines can be made into circles, as we all know. In every situation, the elements to provide solutions for the most difficult problems, exist; we need only perceive them. It is said elsewhere in the *I Ching* that, in the hands of the Creative, everything finds a use. Extended to the relationship between the human being and God, this principle is amplified in *The Ting* (50)*, in the commentary to the first line: "...every person of good will can in some way or other suc-

*Because the English word "caldron" does not seem to be a sufficient equivalent to the Chinese word "ting," I have used "ting." The Ting refers to a vessel used for sacrifice, and to our inner container for spiritual nourishment, which needs to be kept pure and clear of contaminating ideas.

11

ceed. No matter how lowly he may be, provided he is ready to purify himself, he is accepted. He attains a station in which he can prove himself fruitful in accomplishment, and as a result he gains recognition." The Tao knows how to make everything succeed.

Although we live in an external world in which things may be measured and defined, the Tao which governs change in this world arises in the hidden world, and may not be measured or defined. We may approximate it, but our approximations are limited. The Tao is perceptible in the deepest reaches of our inner being, in our intuitive awareness, and in our undifferentiated knowledge of all things.

In using the *I Ching* in self-development, we bring our intuitive knowledge of the Tao, the Unifying Principle, into conscious awareness. This is accomplished through listening to the empty space within, where the origins of our thought processes are able to be perceived. One line of the *I Ching* counsels us to "hold to what is essential and let go of the trivial"; another says, "hold to what endures"; *The Well* (48) counsels that we need to go down to the very well-springs of our being to find the answers. *The Clinging* (30) counsels us to intercept the germinal elements of thought; another hexagram says that the superior man knows "the seeds"; in perceiving the seeds of action, he knows in advance their consequences, therefore he withdraws in time from conflict. To find the seeds of action, to know what is germinal, or what endures, or what is essential, the *I Ching* teaches us to "keep still," in the hexagram *Keeping Still* (52). By keeping still we find the empty space within, where the seeds of our actions exist in our emotions as doubts, desires, and discontents.

In navigating our way across the ocean, we fix our position by having reference to stationary points such as the North Star and the Sun. Not that these heavenly bodies are eternally fixed—but that they endure in their places as far as human life is concerned. If we want to know what endures beyond all things, we find it to be the empty space that lies within every atom; it is out in space, it is here in us. This empty space is the residing place of the Creative and the Tao, the Cosmic Mind and the Cosmic Will. We need do no more than look within and listen within. Lao Tzu said, "Few things under heaven are so instructive as the lessons of Silence, or as beneficial as the fruits of Non-Adoo." Elaborating on this principle, he said, "Thirty spokes converge upon a single hub; it is on the hole in the center that the use of the cart hinges. We make a vessel from a lump of clay; it is the empty space within the vessel that makes it useful. We make doors and windows for a room; but it is these empty spaces that make the room livable. Thus, while the tangible has advantages, it is the intangible that makes it useful."

The hexagrams of the *I Ching* reflect the workings of Tao, or Cosmic Will, not only on the grand cosmic scale but also in the lowliest life circumstance. By consulting them we intercept the images before they become reality; this allows us to change our fate through adapting to the demands of the time. The hexagrams we receive in the chance throwing of coins give us a cross-section of all the tangents of change created by our inner attitudes. Emphasized in the *I Ching* are the far-reaching effects that our attitudes have on others, and whether these attitudes draw beneficial forces from the hidden world to whatever we do, or repel such forces.

Fate, in the *I Ching,* is the trajectory of events that results from elements in our attitudes. If these elements are harmonious with the Cosmic Will, of which our will and inner nature are but emanations, our fate is guided by beneficial influences, because the great Will of the Universe always acts in a beneficial way. If, however, our attitudes are out of harmony, we are not only out of balance within ourselves, we oppose the Cosmic Will, and it can no longer benefit us. In this respect, the Tao is synonomous with the natural law. We understand very well the negative consequences of planting out-of-doors in the winter. Similarly, if our attitudes oppose the natural way, or Cosmic Will, we are subject to the misfortunes that arise as a natural consequence. Such misfortunes are described in the *I Ching* as "attacks of chance," while the traps created by incorrect attitudes are referred to as a "hostile fate." Such a fate is not permanent, but may be reversed or by-passed through changing the patterns that have become engrained as our way of life.

To equalize extremes is part of the natural law. A haughty, pretentious attitude stands like a narrow, steep mountain that is constantly being attacked by the elements; as a consequence, it erodes into the valley. The valley, likewise,

13

because it is a depression, receives all that erodes into it. As Lao Tzu noted, to be empty is to receive; to be full is to suffer loss. Modesty, therefore, because it proceeds from emptiness, is always in harmony with the forces of nature. To counteract a hostile fate, it is essential to cultivate modesty. Perfect modesty, however, is seen to lie between the two extremes of the mountain and the valley. The *I Ching* gives the image of the well-developed personality as the mountain that erodes, filling up the valley to become a plain. In this case the change is brought about by consciously ridding ourselves of pretense and vanity—the mountain—and filling in that which, in us, is too little, such as lack of self-esteem and assurance of inner worth—the valley—to become the plain. This is the image of the 15th hexagram, *Modesty*. Modesty is attained by freeing ourselves of those elements in our attitudes that cause us to be more, or less, than what we are, in our true, original, and good nature. By conscious will, we change these elements, and maintain an on-going conscientiousness to keep ourselves pure in mind; one line describes this as working to brighten our "already bright virtue," another as being modest about our modesty. Impure attitudes are imbalanced and extreme. By following the correct path, we are able to minimize the hostile attacks of chance and draw help from the Creative to accomplish our goals. The correct path, however, lies in the hidden, or inner world, through which it is essential to have a guide. As the second line of *Difficulty at the Beginning* (3) puts it, "If a man tries to hunt in a strange forest and has no guide, he loses his way. When he finds himself in difficulties he must not try to steal out of them unthinkingly and without guidance. Fate cannot be duped; premature effort, without the necessary guidance, ends in failure and disgrace." The *I Ching*, when used daily, acts as such a guide.

In working with the *I Ching* daily, we are made aware that we live on two planes of existence at once, one hidden (an inner world existence) and one evident (an outer world existence). Progress on the inner plane is achieved by meeting moral challenges on the plane of the evident. Through our inner world progress we develop a crystallized light form of ourselves that survives physical death. To bring this light form to maturity and crystallization through self-development is our ultimate Tao, or destiny, To avoid or ignore this destiny is to continually feel dissatisfied and in conflict with life.

To make progress in our inner world existence, we must bring our yang and yin characteristics into the correct order. This ordering and character development is always a matter of choice. The Chinese word for Tao shows a foot guided by a head; the head chooses to go, the foot follows. Tao refers to our inner path, therefore the choice is whether or not to follow the inner way, the guiding light, or lodestar, within. This ordering means that our yang abilities—intuition, ability to perceive truth, inner listening, inner sense of responsibility—must lead our personality, not our yin abilities—learning, intellect, skills, wit, and outer life with its considerations. The embodiments of these yang and yin powers in our personality are respectively called the superior and the inferior man. Self-development is to bring the superior self into mastery of our personality. Order begins when we place first importance on keeping our inmost thoughts and motives correct; disorder begins when we sacrifice the higher values for the sake of the lower, and when we give preeminence to intellect over intuition.

The structure of the hexagrams is based on these principles of ordering. The first, third, and fifth lines, for instance, are seen as superior to the second, fourth, and sixth lines. The top three lines (called the heaven trigram) are seen as superior to the bottom three lines (the earth trigram). The individual lines are either yang, represented by a solid line, or yin, represented by a divided line. When yang lines are in the first, third, and fifth places, and yin lines are in the second, fourth, and sixth places, the hexagram is said to be perfectly ordered. The most ordered hexagram is the 63rd, *After Completion*. The hexagram in which these lines are all reversed is the 64th, *Before Completion*. In the latter hexagram, the lines are all in an ordering such that, with one movement of all six lines upward, with the top line displaced to become the new bottom line, the arrangement becomes that of *After Completion*.

☲ Li	☵ K'an
☵ K'an	☲ Li
Before Completion	*After Completion*

15

The interpretation of the hexagrams has to do not only with the placement of the lines, as shown above, but also with the placement of the lines as three-lined units called trigrams. In the foregoing example, Li, the trigram of light and clarity, is placed on top in *Before Completion,* with K'an, the trigram of toil and danger, placed on the bottom. In *After Completion* the trigrams are reversed. It is said in the interpretation that the ordering of *Before Completion* is not yet correct because clarity (Li) must be the foundation of effort before effort can become successful, as is the case in *After Completion,* when things have been brought to order. In another analogy, the trigram Li represents flames rising upward, giving off light, while the action of K'an, which represents water, is downward. If opposite trends of action are to be meaningful, they must relate: the actions must move toward each other. In *Before Completion,* the action of the top trigram, Li, moves upward and that of the bottom trigram, K'an, moves downward; they don't come to meet, or relate. In *After Completion* they meet and relate, and thus produce success. In the correct ordering, the water is in a pot over the fire, producing steam, or energy.

It is useful to note that many concepts in the *I Ching* differ from traditional Western concepts. For example, we tend to view intuition as a feminine faculty, saying women ought to be intuitive and not necessarily practical, and men ought to be practical and pragmatic and not necessarily intuitive. From the *I Ching* point of view, both men and women have intuitive and intellectual faculties in equal importance because, as human beings, we contain both primal powers in microcosm; neither sexes are meant to exaggerate or deny their intuitive or their intellectual faculties.

Intuition, in the *I Ching,* is our direct perception of the Creative Image that originates in the hidden world. The best analogy is to see the Creative as a *genie,* capable of answering questions of concern. When its answers come, they are often in the form of a sudden insight, or we may hear them. The intellect, with its memory and coordinating abilities, then gives expression to the genie's utterances. Genie, by the way, is the source of the Greek word, genius. According to Webster, it meant "a tutelary spirit that is allotted to every person at his birth, to preside over his destiny in life." It was corrupted in

16

the Age of Reason by the additional implication of "intellectual powers." From the *I Ching* view, a true genius is anyone whose intellect draws upon and conveys the gifts of the genie within, through devotedly placing himself in its proximity. Both Einstein and Mozart freely admitted that they "heard" the messages. Our cultural tendency has been to deny their admission, viewing it as a sort of modesty. That it was, but it was also the truth. The voice we hear within is the same as that of the Sage whom we consult through the *I Ching*.

Until we are familiar with the concepts, it is best to put aside arguments we may find with words such as inferior or superior, masculine or feminine, or any other ideas we may see in a Western orientation. We might assume, for instance, that the masculine principle refers to a macho way of behaving; quite the opposite, it refers to a kingly aspect of mind: generous, tolerant, patient, and self-reliant, not needing to assert itself at all. Similarly, the feminine principle is simply to nourish and rear, to be true and steady, and capable of enduring in a menial position without loss of dignity. The principles of growth and development apply equally to men and to women; situations arise which require responses from either the masculine or the feminine parts of our natures. In respect to the Creative Power, all life stands on the yin, or receptive side of things. To invoke the beneficial action of the Creative, we must exercise the receptive part of our natures. Thus, Lao Tzu wrote, "Know the masculine, keep to the feminine." If we avoid jumping to conclusions, the Creative will unfold in its most enlightening way.

2.

The Lines, Trigrams, and Hexagrams

The Lines

The six lines which make up the hexagrams are either yang or yin lines. Yang lines are derived from odd numbers. All odd numbers are seen as being derived from the number of the Creative, which is the number one. Similarly, all yin lines are seen as being derived from the number two, the number of the Receptive. Yang lines are also called "light lines," being associated with the light power. They are represented by a solid, unbroken line (———) which symbolizes the positive, unbroken power of the Creative. Yin lines are called "dark lines," being associated with the dark, womb-like power of the Receptive, and are divided in the middle (— —), so as to represent the multiplying effect of nurturing, the bringing of the many things into existence. The movement of a yang line is outward (←—→), and at its maximum thrust, it severs in the middle, becoming a yin line. The movement of a yin line is inward (→←), and at its maximum thrust, it merges to become a yang line. It is in this way that all changes complete themselves, initiating an ever-moving wheel of change.

In the throwing of coins, or the dropping of yarrow stalks, either an odd or an even number is obtained; it if is an odd number, a yang line is drawn; if an even number, a yin line is drawn. This is repeated six times until a complete hexagram is drawn.

The Trigrams

Since Yang, as the originating element, has the number one, and Yin, the nurturing element, the number two, their combination and totality have the number three. Three also

18

stands for T'ai Chi—the Primal Unity, the Container of all, the Void. Likewise, three yang or three yin lines represent their respective forces in their totality. Three yang lines form the primary trigram of the Creative, named Ch'ien (☰), and three yin lines form the primary trigram of the Receptive, named K'un (☷). The Chinese liked to think of them as the father and the mother, and to think of their six possible combinations as their children—the eldest, middle, and youngest sons, and the eldest, middle, and youngest daughters—as an easy way of remembering them. It is thought that the trigrams developed from an earlier system of divination which involved simply one yang and one yin line. In the consultation one drew either a yes or no answer, as we flip a coin for a yes or no answer. Three throws, standing for things in their totality, were seen to give more possible meanings, and at a later time, six throws were seen as completing the three dimensions of reality.

The trigrams of the three sons show a single yang line moving up from the bottom position in Chen, the eldest son (☳), to the middle position in K'an, the middle son (☵), to the top position in Ken, the youngest son (☶). Similarly, the yin line proceeds upwards in the trigrams of the daughters, from the bottom place in Sun, the eldest daughter (☴), to the middle place in Li, the middle daughter (☲), to the top place in Tui, the youngest daughter (☱).

Each trigram is seen as having its own special characteristics. The trigram of the father, Ch'ien (☰), represents the unbroken Creative Force. It is the heaven force, therefore it is always beneficial; it is strong and firm. When doubled, with Ch'ien both below and above, it becomes a hexagram, in which the qualities of the trigrams are intensified, or doubled. When the trigram Ch'ien is both below and above, the hexagram is called *The Creative*. It is the first hexagram in the *I Ching*, and represents the action of the deity as the all-powerful force enduring through time.

The trigram of the mother, K'un (☷), symbolizes receptivity, the devoted, the earth, the yielding, the soft, and the nourishing. Doubled into a hexagram, it represents the earth in the sense of enduring what is put upon it, and in the sense of top-soil, which, without doing anything more than

19

allowing itself to be acted upon by the elements, gives rise to all the things that grow from it and depend upon it for their nourishment. Compared to Ch'ien, K'un represents the womb-like power of the dark. It is the second hexagram in the *I Ching.*

Chen (☳), the eldest son, shows the yang line beginning its ascent as powerful thrust; it is movement and thunder. When it stands doubled, its powerful thrust is doubled, therefore, as a hexagram, it is called *Shock* (51).

K'an (☵), the middle son, signifies water—active water as in white water, rushing water, falling water, and rain. It is water that pushes wheels and produces energy as steam; it is water at work. The meanings associated with K'an are work, or toiling, and, because water unhesitatingly plunges over precipices, danger. In psychological terms, it is the danger of working hard and not seeing any results. It is the danger of having ambition and being thwarted. In its doubled form as a hexagram, it is called *The Abysmal,* subtitled *Danger* (29).

Ken (☶), the youngest son, shows the yang line at the top, near the clouds. It is the image of a mountain as a place where streams flow and birds sing, a place of solitude and serenity, a place of forests. It contains hidden treasures, such as seams of coal or gold, and it gives nourishment to all the land around because it absorbs rain and holds water that flows down to the lake, watering everything on its way. The ideal mountain is one with a lake on top which continually feeds everything below. When Ken is doubled, the resulting hexagram is called *Keeping Still* (52), and it refers to a particular meditative state of mind.

The eldest daughter, Sun (☴), has the image of wind penetrating through cracks and of wood penetrating through the soil as roots; it is the gentle which succeeds by adapting and going around obstacles. It is also the wind dispersing things, as in dispersing waves into foam. Psychologically, it is gentleness that disperses hardness and anger. Doubled into a hexagram, it is called the *Gentle,* subtitled *The Penetrating, Wind* (57), and we find that it often refers to the way truth gently penetrates the cracks in our mental defenses to become recognizable perceptions. The proverbial light comes on in our minds and we understand.

Li (☲), the middle daughter, has the image of fire dependent on wood, which causes it to burn. (Wood, in the *The Ting* (50), symbolizes character, which, in *Development* (53), takes a long time to grow.) The flame, in its dependence and docility, is able to give off light. When Li is doubled into a hexagram, it is called *The Clinging* (30), and means leading through being led. It means attaining and holding on to clarity of mind through the cultivation of docility and detachment. As long as we are emotionally attached to things, we cannot see with clarity; in detachment we attain clarity. Through this clear view we find correct solutions, and thereby are able to lead and aid others.

Tui (☱), the youngest daughter, has the image of a shining lake which symbolizes joyousness. It is joy associated with the quiet peacefulness of still water. Because it is also associated with autumn and the joy of harvest, it is also imbued with a certain melancholy because of winter's coming. As lake water, it shines and reflects as if metallic. It is also water as fog, low-lying vapor, swamp water, and stagnant water. Doubled into a hexagram, it is called *The Joyous,* subtitled *Lake* (58), and contains all the concepts of joy, ranging from joy as serenity to joy as pursuit of sensual pleasure. Psychologically, it calls for seeing the difference between that which brings peace and inner harmony and that which brings suffering.

The Hexagrams

By placing one trigram on top another, and observing how their characteristics affect each other, hexagrams are formed and interpreted. Certain trigrams, such as the heaven trigram, are seen to "move upwards," while others, such as the earth trigram, move downwards; each move toward their own sphere. Opposite moving trigrams arouse each other only if their movements "come to meet." This condition occurs in the 11th hexagram, *Peace,* in which Ch'ien is below, moving upward, and K'un is above, moving downward; thus, they come to meet; blessing and enrichment result. In the 12th hexagram, *Standstill (Stagnation),* their order is reversed; each moves into its own sphere and they do not relate. In psychological terms, peace occurs only when people are

21

receptive and open-minded toward one another; then an influence for the good can occur. When standstill takes place, people are not receptive to each other and the only thing to do is to withdraw and wait until the time changes. Withdrawal, being the correct response, initiates a change back toward peace. K'an, the middle son, representing water, arouses Li, the middle daughter, which represents fire, but only when they are placed in a complementary relationship. When fire is above water, the two do not relate, but when fire is beneath water, as when fire heats water into steam and produces energy, something is achieved. Chen, the eldest son, representing thunder, and Sun, the eldest daughter, representing wind, are seen as arousing and strengthening one another. The youngest son, Ken, representing the mountain, and the youngest daughter, Tui, representing the lake, feed one another: the lake gives off mists that rise up to the mountain; in turn, the mists become rain which flows back down to the lake.

Of the several methods of consulting the *I Ching,* the commonest and easiest is to throw coins. The head side of the coin represents the yang force. The yang force is given the value of three—that of T'ai Chi, as including both Yang and Yin. The tail side represents the yin force, and has the value of two. (Some writers have assigned Yang to the tail side and Yin to the head side, but this seems inappropriate since Yang is related to the mind and the head and Yin to the things created. (Things are usually pictured on the tail sides of coins.) The Sage, we may note, relates to whichever way we use the coins.) While any coin can be used, pennies have the appropriateness of having the primal value one, and represent the underlying common denominator of all other numbers and values. In this lowliest position, the penny is like the water at the bottom of the well, which symbolizes truth. Pennies also symbolize simplicity and humility, the attitudes needed for communicating with the great Sage, and the attitudes most highly prized in the *I Ching.*

Three coins are thrown down in random fashion and their values as heads (3) and tails (2) are added up. There are four possible combinations:

All heads 3 3 3 equaling nine—yang line

All tails	2	2	2	equaling six—yin line
Two heads, one tail	3	3	2	equaling eight—yin line
Two tails, one head	3	2	2	equaling seven—yang line

The first throw of coins creates the bottom, or beginning line, the second throw the second line from the bottom, the third throw the next one up, and so on to the sixth, or top, line.

When we throw all heads or all tails, these unusual combinations are regarded as specially significant and are called "changing lines." The flow of energy from Yang to Yin and from Yin back to Yang resembles an electrical circuit, in which the energy flows from positive to negative pole and back again. When the yang energy reaches its maximum thrust, the yin polarity takes over, drawing the energy to itself; reaching its maximum, it then reflects the energy back again towards the yang pole, where once again, the pull of the yang force takes over. The maximum point for either the yang or the yin influence is the point of change towards the opposite pole. A throw of all heads symbolizes this point of change of the yang force. Likewise, a throw of all tails symbolizes the point of change for the yin force. Changing lines are seen as "unresolved" lines which reflect unresolved elements in our situations; these lines must be changed to their opposites to become resolved, and in changing them, a new hexagram is created. The new hexagram shows the direction in which the situation is moving, thus we are able to obtain a complete perspective. If we throw only sevens or eights, we obtain a single hexagram; if we throw any sixes or nines, only these lines are changed, with the sevens or eights remaining the same, to form the second hexagram.

If we obtain only one hexagram by throwing the coins, we are meant to read the material only to the beginning of the explanation of the individual lines. If we have not received sixes or nines, the individual lines have no special significance for us, and the hexagram is meant to be contemplated as a whole. The lines may be read in their totality to understand the way movement takes place in a hexagram, but for most purposes, it is sufficient to read everything but the "lines." If we throw sixes or nines, it is meant that we also read the changing lines they have created. For example, if we have a six in the third place, we read all material to the beginning of the lines, then we read the third line and its commentary. After reading all lines that are formed by sixes or nines, we then change these lines to their opposites. If they were yang lines, we make them into yin lines, and vice versa. These, we put into the new hexagram, along with the yang and yin lines formed by throws of seven or eight which we do not change. The new hexagram, formed in this manner, is contemplated as helping to define the meaning of the first hexagram. *Splitting Apart* (23) changes to *Deliverance* (40) when the first, fifth, and sixth lines of *Splitting Apart* are changing lines. The first line describes doubt beginning in one's mind; the fourth line mentions that the "splitting apart" caused by doubt has already reached its peak; the top line says that the splitting apart has reached its end and the seed of good remains to grow anew; deliverance is already in its beginnings, because doubt is being contained. Such a sequence refers more to a situation that has been taking place and is now ending, with a new beginning in view. *Deliverance* counsels that the new beginning must be secured through recuperating in peace and keeping still.

Once a hexagram has been drawn, we may refer to the key included in the appendix of the *I Ching* (Wilhelm translation), to obtain the hexagram's number. The upper trigram of our hexagram is looked up on the horizontal row of trigrams at the top of the key, while our lower trigram is looked up on the column of trigrams at the left side of the key; the point on the key where the vertical line from our upper trigram and the horizontal line from our lower trigram intersect, gives us the number of the hexagram. After finding the hexagram in Book I, it is wise to compare it with the one we have drawn, to avoid errors.

Having drawn a hexagram or a hexagram set, we have what might be thought of as a subject heading for any further hexagrams we may draw at one sitting. All the hexagrams will refer to the same subject until we completely understand what is being said. If we misconstrue what the hexagram is talking about, it will continue on the same subject, making us rethink the matter. We may even get identical hexagrams and lines, indicating that we have not yet understood the message. Although it is thought by some people that the Sage does not like to be asked the same question twice, and that to repeat the question is to importune, this view applies only if we are of a hostile or testing mood. The *I Ching* will have nothing to do with our arrogance or egotism, but it will answer and carry on a conversation with our inner thoughts as long as we are sincere in trying to understand. Furthermore, it is important to give it enough space to allow it to answer fully. A complete conversation seems to occur when we have received six hexagrams (or six sets of hexagrams), although three sets of hexagrams are generally all that a beginner is able to absorb. Once we have completely understood a message, as in six sets of hexagrams, then we may ask questions on less important matters; the replies to these questions are usually complete in a single hexagram set.

Some hexagrams show the time of our situation; for example, we may be advised not to act now because of unbalanced elements in our attitude. Hexagrams will often indicate situations about to occur, giving us counsel to help us meet the situation with a correct attitude. Just as often the messages discuss a situation that has just happened, in order that we may put it into perspective.

Sometimes we are blocked from perceiving the answers by rigid elements in our attitude. At such a time we may experience a shocking event which is then followed by getting the hexagram *Shock* (51). The *I Ching* informs us that "shock is good," because shocking events tend to weaken the hold that false ideas have on our minds. Shock is used as a teaching tool only when there is no other way to break through such obdurate blockages.

Sometimes we get a hexagram in which all the lines are changing lines. This causes the hexagram to appear contradictory. However, it simply indicates that several choices exist, some superior and some inferior. It is simply that we must choose. Having many changing lines in the same hexagram may show us the way a situation progresses, so that we may know how to adapt to it as it happens.

When we are confronted with problems of apparent contradiction between lines, it is best if we keep our minds open to allow the correct perception to materialize. We understand the *I Ching* better if we put ourselves in the position of the Sage. On being consulted for advice, we find we are restricted to pointing to one of 64 hexagrams which are written in an archaic language unfamiliar to the person we are trying to answer. One hexagram is too restrictive to convey our meaning while another is too general. However, if the person consulting us does not hold us too strictly to the language of the hexagram, if he does not try to make us shape our reply too rigidly to the framework of his question, and if he simply lets the answer penetrate his conscious mind by suggestion, he will surely begin to understand. But if he is impatient, or if he seeks only the reply that suits him, or subjects everything we say to rigid intellectual analysis, our suggestions will not penetrate, however earnestly we try to communicate with him.

The replies given in a series of hexagrams contain a line of thought, just as in music a line of melody is interwoven among chords and rhythmical beats. In a series of three hexagrams, for instance, the word *limitation* may crop up repeatedly, indicating that we need to set limits on our actions or the ideas we entertain. If, through keeping our minds open and unstructured, we allow it to happen, the line of thought emerges intuitively as an insight. By "allowing it" is meant that we do not stand by impatiently watching and waiting for the answer. The Sage will not respond to impatience, desire, or expectation, but only acts as a free agent, unharnessed by our will. The humility of asking for help to understand, unfailingly brings about a breakthrough of the meaning.

Although our relationship with the Sage is thoroughly treated in the third section of this book, it is part of this overview to mention that we begin to be aware, through consulting the Sage regularly, that we are communicating with a distinct personality which is very consistent in its way of relating to us, and in its views. We find that whatever question we ask, it will speak only on matters that really concern us. If our concern is about money, it will address that concern; if we think it is discussing something else, we are simply not understanding it. If we think, however, that this Sage will take over and solve our problems, we misjudge it; it is likely, instead, to speak of the danger of self-pity, or tell us that it is unproductive to "look upwards" for help; while it will help us, we must do our part by disciplining our inferior nature and by putting our life together through our own efforts. If we feel hostile to this personality, we find that it simply disappears, becoming incommunicative. When we have a correct attitude towards it, we are nourished and supported by the messages, and we feel a certain friendly and helpful presence in it. However, if we persist in going our own way and ignore its advice, it is likely to say, the next time we consult it, that "the teacher, when confronted with such entangled folly, has no other course but to leave the fool to himself for a time, not sparing him the humiliation that results. This is frequently the only means of rescue." While the Sage is tolerant of our ignorance, is forbearing with our arrogance, and demands nothing of us, we are nevertheless made aware that the *I Ching* is not a toy or parlor game but a means of communicating with a higher being, and of discovering the secrets of the higher world of the spirit and the great truths of life. Indeed, what better source can one find for such knowledge and wisdom than the Source itself!

3.

The Superior and Inferior Elements
of Personality

In Book II of the *I Ching* it is said that at the dawn of consciousness we stand within pre-existing systems of relationships; in their totality, these relationships comprise the Cosmic Order. For example, the planets orbit around the sun, creating the seasons; the moon orbits around the earth, creating the tides; life on earth fits within these larger systems of relationships, for we cannot plant without regard to the seasons, or navigate without regard to the tides. Heaven, as the larger system, determines the lesser systems; as systems, they do not combat, but complement each other. As these systems move, one within the other, they move in accordance with the overall principles of ordering; change—the natural movement of things within pre-existing relationships—follows definite laws. These laws comprise the Cosmic Will, the great Tao of the universe. They are seen to move in ways that are beneficial and harmonious to the existence of the whole. The *I Ching* mirrors this ordering, thus mirrors the great Tao.

Deviations from the Cosmic Order occur when the trajectories of change are disrupted mechanically from outside. In the human sphere, disruptions come from acting in conflict with our true, original nature, an example of which is the consciously perpetrated unkind act. Misfortune is the natural result. In *I Ching* terms, although the misfortune may be no more than a subjective feeling of being disappointed in oneself, it is also a disappointment that accrues to the entire universe in subtle ways beyond our immediate recognition. The accumulation of disorder, or misfortune, amounts to a sort of karmic quantity that can only be reversed by sustained work towards the good.

Deviations from the Cosmic Order may also occur when we do a right-seeming thing at a wrong time. In defrosting a refrigerator, it is better to wait for the ice to soften than to chip away at it when solidly frozen. It is the essence of wisdom and order to do appropriate things at appropriate times. Disorders and misfortunes caused by contrary actions, for the most part, may be repaired simply by ceasing to do them, but when such misfortunes occur because of entrenched habits of mind, it is necessary to gradually free oneself of those habits. A great part of our work with the *I Ching* consists of correcting defective habits of mind in order to rescue situations that have gone awry.

In our personality, disorder begins when we put a higher value on our intellect (yin faculty) than on our intuition (yang faculty). When our intellect leads, it by-passes its true function of serving and bringing forth the products of intuitive insight. The true purpose of our intellect is to train our body—as in playing the piano, or as in dressing ourselves; it enables us to commit things to memory, and to coordinate information; the intellect also engages in making simple decisions, but it deviates from its true purpose and usurps command of our personality when it begins to program our life into set responses. Instead of being open and receptive—attuned to our intuition—we become closed and defensive. As the false leader of our personality, the I Ching calls it "the inferior man." The inferior man may succeed for a time, but even his greatest success is a meteoric rise that is doomed to becoming a meteoric fall, because such a rise is against the natural order, and all trajectories of change are inherently in conflict with it. Hitler stands as an example of the meteoric rise and fall of the inferior man.

In working with the *I Ching* we learn to identify the superior and inferior aspects of our personality; this helps us reinforce our intuitive awareness and restore the natural balance of our true nature. In the hexagrams, dominance of the superior and of the inferior man are held in contrast as alternative courses of action; our choices, our acts, and our decisions of the moment lead either toward harmony with ourselves, which the *I Ching* calls 'success', or against that harmony, which the *I Ching* calls 'misfortune'. This success or misfortune is seen to accrue to become an overall life pattern; the success of the moment amounts to a step along the road of spiritual development, while misfortune is a step

29

along the false path that leads only to a dead-end. The firmly established, well-developed superior man is in such fundamental harmony with the beneficial power of the Creative that all things work to his benefit. His will, being attuned to the Cosmic Will, cannot fail; the *I Ching* says that the superior man succeeds in everything he does with the "inevitability of natural law." Indeed, "all oracles are bound to concur in his success."

When the superior man occupies the ruling place in our personality, the regenerative power of the Creative is activated. Just by being in the right place, the superior man initiates and precipitates beneficial action. The Creative Power works through the medium of time, therefore the superior man abides in his place with constancy; constancy "precipitates" the creative image into existence. Throughout the *I Ching* we encounter the concept of "bringing things to completion", which means that all creative work is achieved through inner firmness, steadiness in inner direction, devotion to what is good, and constancy in maintaining these attitudes. Constancy, in following the good, has the ultimate power.

The inferior man, which exists only when it occupies the superior man's place, is capable of incorporating the power of the dark force, which is that of degeneration, decay, and death. The dark power arises only because we doubt the Creative as the power of good. Doubt is the dark force. It is not a quiescent, but a fully active power. When we engage in doubting that by following the good we will find our life's meaning, we not only keep the Creative Force from being activated, but we activate the power of the dark force, with its obstructions, traps, and adversities. This negative force sets off adverse trends of action that must run their course until we correct the negative elements in our attitudes. It is as if to say there is a Cosmic Law against achieving the good through doubtful means, and that good may issue only from good. As long as the inferior man rules within us, an inner conflict, or "war," is set off within our personality; our superior man is held captive by our inferior man. Until we restore order, our personality remains fundamentally split. The inferior man may hold the superior man captive for a long time, but, as long as a person is alive, both potentials exist within him.

30

The work of self-development is to resolve all internal rifts, restoring the personality to wholeness, or oneness, in harmony with the Tao. The causes of illness that have their roots in internal conflict, gradually abate and become eradicated; the person is restored to health and well-being. The causes of conflict with others that also have their roots in personal conflict, are eradicated; the person lives at peace with himself and with others. Because of the far reaching consequences of correcting the fundamental elements in our attitudes, the *I Ching* pays attention to the "germinal," emphasizes the "essential," and goes down to the very wellsprings of our attitudes: for it is there that a person chooses to follow either the superior or the inferior man within; it is there that he accepts or rejects the doubts offered by others and so sets himself on a course in life.

We are informed in one hexagram that even the inferior man seeks what is right; that is, his fundamental goal is to find and fulfill his purpose, which is to serve our higher nature. However, when the inferior man leads, he assumes the superior man's goal, that of attaining immortality, to be his own—something that can never be, for the superior goal can only be attained by the superior man. In pursuit of this goal, the inferior man uses inferior means; he thinks only of the goal and how he can contrive to reach it, whereas the superior man fixes his attention on seeing that his path is correct; he hardly thinks of the goal, therefore he reaches it involuntarily, because of his way of life. His path leads directly to it.

The Superior Man

The superior man represents the highest potential expression of the original good elements of our personality. It is what we are, intrinsically, if we do not disrupt the natural order by following the inferior aspects of our personality.

Each of the 64 hexagrams has a section entitled "The Image," which describes some aspect of the superior man. In the first hexagram the image says, "The superior man makes himself strong and untiring." In the second hexagram, the image says, "The superior man who has breadth of character carries the outer world." In the third, it says, "The superior man brings order out of confusion," and so on, in all but three hexagrams. At the same time, the inferior man, often pluralized, is described in the hexagram lines as attitudes, or as trends of thought or action which undermine the superior man.

Aspects of character associated with the superior man are the will toward good, kindness, devotion, openness, detachment, innocence, and modesty. These qualities are contained in our original pure nature; in the superior man they are bonded together with perseverance.

Our will toward the good is expressed in our willingness to accept the life-situation in which we find ourselves, and to make the best of it, while keeping a just and moderate view of all things. This willingness is an acceptance that causes the person who suddenly finds himself in the water, to somehow swim rather than drown. This willingness also means to play our part in the life-drama cheerfully, accepting the part assigned to us, and allowing ourselves to be acted upon. It is the opposite of a demanding, egocentric attitude which collapses when adversity strikes. This will toward the good is also expressed in our natural attraction to what is essential and correct.

Kindness, one *I Ching* line explains, springs from "inner necessity." It is a part of the original innocence of our nature to be kind; we have to plan and program ourselves to be otherwise. On seeing a child about to run in front of a car, we automatically move to rescue it. Only afterwards does our inferior self enter to take credit, or see any advantage in our having done it. If an animal runs in front of our automobile, it is natural to avoid hitting it. To steer towards it requires that we must previously have made a pact with our inferior self to put aside caring, for some reason or other. It is against our nature to kill, therefore, in police and military work, it is necessary to repeatedly train people to overcome these inhibitions. That is why silhouettes of people are often used on police shooting ranges.

Similarly, it is in our nature to be honest. To do a dishonest thing we must first create a "reasonable pretext." We create such pretexts out of fear and from doubt that the situation will work out if we do the correct thing. This is why, from the *I Ching* point of view, if we have to justify an act, the act is likely to be wrong.

Openness is also part of our natural honesty. To adopt fixed attitudes it is necessary first to accept rationales and beliefs which close off other possible ways of seeing or doing things. This process too, we do out of fear—fear that another way of seeing things may expose us to risk; we take refuge in the fixed idea as a barricade against the unknown. Once we have created rationales, or have taken refuge in fixed ideas, it is very difficult to give them up. Rationales seem to take on a life of their own, and only a strong act of will can liberate us from their hold.

Modesty refers to an awareness of that which is higher than ourself—we respect the unknown and recognize the insufficiency of our inferior powers. It means we are determined to be led rather than to lead, that we will flow with events rather than resist them, and that we will remain unstructured in mind rather than defend ourself with fixed ideas. It means that we maintain a certain humility so that we protect our dignity as a sacred trust, and do not sacrifice our higher nature for the sake of our lower nature. This sort of modesty, founded on a continuing conscientiousness, accords with our true, original nature.

When as children we observed someone hurting an animal or bullying a child, we felt sympathy for the injured one and embarrassment because the other person was violating his own nature. The child's naturally detached response has the unique quality of reflecting back the deed to the doer, causing him to see himself. When he learns blame, guilt, and vindictiveness, and "gives up" on the person doing the wrong thing, he simply causes that person to become hardened in his sense of humiliation; that person justifies himself and continues doing it. However, the superior man's response has a good effect on the wrong-doer, without his consciously intending it. Children are naturally moral, modest, and detached in the beginning. The natural modesty of the child is wordless and lacking in self-justifications. Such justifications and comparisons are the activity of the inferior man within.

Perseverance is a quality that we possibly have at birth, but one which it is essential to develop once we have lost our natural innocence, for it is the glue needed to hold our superior aspects of character together. Without perseverance, doubt undermines one or another of these aspects, weakening their coordinated effect so that all collapse.

A child perseveres in learning to eat, crawl, and walk, but does not think of it as perseverance. He simply fulfills his nature by continuing in the learning process, step-by-step. However, once we consciously have the goal of learning to walk, as after being hospitalized, we focus on that goal to the point where everything we do is seen as reflecting on it. This focusing is a conscious intervention that makes it necessary to realize that we must be patient and proceed, step-by-step. This exercise of our will to be patient is perseverance. To accomplish our goal we must neither lose sight of it nor keep it so much in mind that our progress is collapsed by each setback. When a child falls he doesn't think, as an adult might, "I'll never learn to walk," thereby jeopardizing his will to learn. Loss of this childlike innocence is a great setback for us. To compensate, we must persevere, maintaining our innocence in a conscious way. Thus, the *I Ching* says again and again, "perseverance furthers." Maintaining conscious innocence entails keeping the forces of doubt and fear from our inner view. We avoid "looking to the side" in envious awareness of the progress of others; we avoid measuring each step, "feeling good" with progress and "miserable" with setbacks; we avoid expecting rewards for our effort, and the tendency, when such rewards are not forthcoming, to rail at Fate as a deliverer of harsh punishments. By keeping our inner view innocent, like that of a child, we are able to achieve the humility and cheerful forward progress that wins the powerful help of the Creative, whereby our goal may effortlessly be achieved.

Virtually all these aspects of character are included in this idea of innocence. In the hexagram *Innocence* (25), the superior man is described as "guileless." "His mind is natural and true, unshadowed by reflection or ulterior designs. For wherever conscious purpose is to be seen, there the truth and innocence of nature have been lost. Nature that is not directed by the spirit is not true, but degenerate nature." Innocence also contains the idea that spontaneous responses, if they are not spoiled by previously made pacts or conscious purpose, are in harmony with the Creative. Such natural responses are always good, kind, modest, and are made possible by a detached and open mind. We do not pre-plan such responses by anticipating what lies ahead, or structure them on the basis of what has happened before. We do not respond conditionally by reference to what others do or fail to do, but solely answer the moment as the moment demands. If our response is influenced by stored-up anger, or desire, or fixed ideas, then it cannot be a response arising from innocence. Innocence is a state which allows us to be acted upon by the higher power. We become a conduit through which the higher power can be expressed; how this power expresses itself is something we cannot know in advance. The response may show itself as anger, but we feel none; it may show itself as wit, or wisdom, or as tenderness, or in the field of action, as great ability, but it is always as if we have not, in and of ourselves, done it. By cultivating innocence, we cultivate those aspects of character that are realized in the enlightened and stabilized true self—the superior man within.

Innocence leads to insight. Our superior self is that which is capable of looking at and listening to what is going on in either the external world or the internal world. The word intuition comes from the Latin word meaning to *look upon* or *into,* and a *sight* and *mental view.* Innocence is thus related to the word *insight.* People who can hear within are called psychics, but, in truth, we all have this ability; it is simply suppressed in most of us. Through inner listening we can also become aware of other people's conscious thoughts. Our superior self listens and looks, but does not speak. What we receive from the inner world that we perceive and know as intuition comes from inside and apart from ourselves, just as what we see of the outer world is outside and apart from ourselves. What we hear within comes from the teacher, the same Sage who speaks through the *I Ching.* It knows the way and comes to help. We can only hear it when we maintain emptiness, innocence, and receptivity. When we jump to conclusions because of fear and impatience, we can't hear the quiet suggestions of the Sage within.

When we say a thing "comes totally out of the blue," this is an intuitive way of saying that we are helped by the Sage. We say "out of the blue," because our words have the clarity of the sky and come from nowhere. What we say is what needs to be said and is perfectly appropriate. Innocence and emptiness make it possible; we are noticably free of emotional attachment and our words come in the vernacular of the moment; everyone understands and agrees. When this happens we are always a bit surprised. The fact is, we are not in possession of such moments, although we make them happen through being in a complementary relationship with the Creative Power. This we can do only through cultivating our superior man within.

The gift of insight differs from person to person. With Mozart it was the gift of hearing and composing music; with Einstein it was that of perceiving the fundamental principles of physics and numbers; with Escoffier it was a gift with food. Others are gifted as parents, carpenters, potters, cabinet makers, actors. Some have mechanical genius or electronic wizardry; others have a gift for getting along with people. Everyone is given gifts which he may bring to the arena of life. Here and there a true wise man may be disguised as a mechanic or common laborer. In his anonymous position of serving people he may have a monumental impact on their lives, without their being aware of it until later. This is the anonymity of the Sage. His gifts are everywhere, and greatest where they are least expected to be. All these gifts are equally valuable, equally necessary to the meaning of life. Everyone is bringing them forth, and they are part of the interweaving of a beautiful design. The divine manifests itself in human beings; it also manifests itself in sunshine, in running water, in still water, in mountains, in valleys, in trees, in birds, in stones, in everything all the time. Lao Tzu wrote:

> The Great Tao is universal like a flood.
> How can it be turned to the right or to the left?
>
> All creatures depend on it,
> And it denies nothing to anyone.
>
> It does its work,
> But it makes no claims for itself.
>
> It clothes and feeds all,
> But it does not lord it over them:
> Thus, it may be called "the Little."

All things return to it as to their home,
But it does not lord it over them:
Thus, it may be called "the Great."

It is just because it does not wish to be great
That its greatness is fully realized.

Then again, in another stanza,

Tao never makes any ado,
And yet it does everything.

And again,

The Tao is hidden and nameless;
Yet it alone knows how to render help and to fufill.

The love of what is good is so much a part of our nature
that to instruct us in it causes us to doubt. The idea of
teaching children "commandments" for following the good
implies that it is not in their nature to follow the good. To
need to make an effort to do what one already does, is not only unnecessary, it has the worse effect of making us doubt our
own goodness, and doubt our love of good. It would make
more sense if we told children the following: "In being true to
your nature you will eventually, through insight, come to love
God with all your heart because you will see the great and
total goodness within you that is also God." To think of this
otherwise, as in "thou must," is not to know that love. When
we must strive to do what we "ought," our inferiors feel envious of others who do not; we become righteousness, condemn
others, create factions, and turn away from innocence: in
such attitudes a whole vortex of darkness operates. The
superior man holds consciously to innocence to preserve the
good that is within himself.

We begin to see, in working daily with the *I Ching,* that
through culturalization, we have assimilated doubts about
our innate goodness and our natural awareness of right and
wrong that comes through our intuition; in doubting our
intuition, we have given power and credibility to the decadent
attitudes and conventions that exist in society. Our intuition,
because of this culturalization, becomes suspended and
inoperative; the result is that our superior nature remains in
only a partially developed state, while our inferior self leads

and dominates our life. Self-development reawakens and strengthens our intuitive awareness, making it possible, once more, to return to our innate goal of bringing our superior nature to maturity.

Until we consult the Sage, we may never have realized that some of the cultural traditions we have taken for granted as true, are decadent and destructive from the viewpoint of the Sage; we may never have realized that while we were living what we thought to be a good pattern of life, that we were cultivating a number of subtle self-flatteries. Nor may we have been aware that the faint feeling of dissatisfaction we have had with life comes from not having fulfilled our higher natures. Many of us are simply too indolent to see any reason to purify ourselves. Most often, we seek to do so only after we have crashed into that great obstuction the *I Ching* calls Fate. Then we realize that something is amiss, and come to suspect that our self-confidence may have no real basis. Only at this point may we be open-minded enough to seek the guidance offered by the great Sage, or to take our spiritual development seriously. How many of us, on getting to this point in life, have experienced that repetitious dream of being in a school where we have not attended any classes, but are suddenly faced with the final exam? It is not that a dire end awaits us, but that we will have missed our great opportunity; we suspect that nothing of any enduring benefit will have been realized from having lived, and we feel regret. We would like to have done things differently—to have fully realized our great potential, to have carefully and lovingly attended the light within (that bit of the divine within), to have let it grow and become fully realized, able to nourish and provide strength for others. This would have been in harmony with our true nature.

While it was free choice that carried us away from our original innocence and allowed us to languish in spiritual indolence, we realize that it is only through going away from oneself and languishing thus, that we awaken one day to realize anything. It is only through returning, by force of will and by choice, that we fully experience the powers of the dark and light within ourselves. Only by overcoming the pull while in the vortex of the dark power do we come out into the light to see the meaning of our existence. This going away from ourselves is necessary; it is part of the course, part of our growth. This is a life for going out and for returning; the light and the dark are there for us to be able to see. Thus the *I Ching* says, "the highest good is to know how to become free of blame," not simply *to be* free of blame.

We may choose to follow our destiny to fulfill our Tao, or not; probably we have to come back into this life cycle again and again until the day we decide to fulfill it. Then we must follow the solitary path in search of clarity, for it is easy to follow what we see with clarity. The *I Ching* is a lantern given us for this search.

The Inferiors

At birth, we have both superior and inferior aspects of nature. The inferior aspects are called inferior because they are inferior in function to the superior aspects. They originate in our bodily needs and may be thought of as our emotional body, or our body-intelligence. It is as if every cell in our bodies is able to communicate its needs in a larger, organized way. Thus, when a series of impulses come from our cells signalling that their fuel and oxygen supplies are getting depleted, we get a feeling that expresses itself as an emotional message: "I am hungry."

In its original meaning, the word emotion meant to move away in the sense of reacting to somthing; later it came to mean stirring or being agitated or affected by something. The emotional body, or body-intelligence, simply reacts, constituting a simple-minded intelligence. As such, it is blind, not being connected to cognition, or recognition. The inferiors mentioned in the *I Ching* are those feelings that register as pain, hunger, thirst, or fatigue, and give rise to a feeling of urgency to "do something." The urgency of their expression may be tamed by cognition. For example, we may be hungry, but in recognizing that we are about to eat, our urgency is contained. The fact that cognition can hold the inferiors in check confirms the view that they comprise a simple intelligence. The influence of cognition is not direct, but is conveyed by an aspect of our superior nature—that of patience, which calms the inferiors by reassuring them that they will be fed. If we listen closely, we can hear this calming action on the part of our patience. However, if it appears that food may be a long time in coming, whether or not the inferiors may be contained depends upon the degree to which we have developed the aspect of patience, and to the degree in which the inferiors have invested their belief in the superior self as leader of the personality. When the inferiors lack confidence in the superior self, fear intrudes and the response becomes more and more hysterical. The inferiors exert great pressure to do something (anything) to allieviate their sense of being threatened; worse, they readily seize upon any apparent solution to the problem, even though this solution might entail compromising the integrity and safety of the personality as a whole. This happens because the inferiors do not see things as a whole; lacking cognition, they are not equipped to lead the personality; when they take over, the personality is bound to be placed in jeopardy. Then, whether or not things work out is entirely due to chance.

Seen in meditation experiences, the inferiors are dwarf-sized characters with childish personalities, not unlike the seven dwarfs of "Snow White," who are undisciplined when left to themselves, living in a state of purposelessness and disarray. In my meditations I have found them to be a nuisance, occupying my inner space with observations and exclamations about everything in sight, and singing ditties that repeat in my mind like a broken record. On one of the first occasions that I saw them, I saw myself on a ship much like that of Columbus's, with the entire crew in rebellion about my "sailing off into nowhere with this *I Ching* thing." They were so occupied with looking at the difficulties of my life at the time and my "not doing anything about them," that the ship (my ship) which they were supposed to be attending, was in a state of total disrepair; it was clear that if I did not take them in hand, the next storm was sure to sink us. Since my *I Ching* guidance had forewarned me to marshall my armies against myself, I saw that the only thing to do was to kill the entire crew, which I did. (This sort of thing is permissible in meditation experiences, as a way of dealing with rebellious and obdurate inferiors.) When I next saw my ship (in meditation some time later) it was repaired and I had a new, neat, and disciplined crew.

As a necessary part of our personality, the inferiors are

good only if disciplined and kept in the proper relationship to the superior self. Obviously, only we can discipline our inner self, and to do that we must first see such discipline as essential to achieving our goals. Body-intelligence is what makes a carpenter able (after practice) to hit the nail instead of his thumb. The pianist teaches the body inferiors (his hands) to play thousands upon thousands of musical notes and patterns which they then remember; the intellect supervises the coordination of the hands and the beat; the superior self within listens to the musical line, and, through this listening, communicates the sense of music to these lower aspects of the personality, which, in turn, give it expression. Without the hands or intellect—functions of the body-intelligence, nothing could be done; without the ability to listen within, the greatness of the music could not be expressed. In fulfilling its role, the body-intelligence receives its due in being recognized; serving the higher self in accomplishing the higher goals of the personality is its true and enduring source of happiness. However, if the overall purpose becomes that of gratifying the body self's need for gratification, a momentary, egotistical thrill may be experienced, but this thrill is always at the expense of the superior self; ultimately, even this thrill does not satisfy, for it dissipates to a vague feeling of dissatisfaction in the deflation that always follows a high feeling.

The amount of self-doubt we learn in growing up determines to what extent our inferiors may undermine and overthrow our superior aspects of character. By the time we encounter the *I Ching*, many of our inferiors will have become powerful as habits of mind and as programmed reactions to circumstances. The lines of the *I Ching* address these programmed responses and the pacts we have made with ourselves to do or not to do things in given situations; these pacts operate as defenses against the Unknown, and arise from mistrust of the Creative, and the fear that it will not be there to help us when we need it.

Many hexagrams and lines refer to the invasion by the inferior element into the superior man's place. In *The Army* (7), when the inferiors lead, defeat is said to be inevitable, hence the army "carries corpses in the wagon." In *Standstill* (12) it is said, "Owing to the influence of the inferior men,

41

mutual mistrust prevails...." In *The Power of the Great* (34) it is said, "the inferior man works through power." In *The Joyous* (58), because of "keeping company with inferior people we are tempted by pleasures inappropriate for the superior man." In *Coming to Meet* (44), "the principle of darkness ascends," as "the rise of the inferior element." These inferiors are thoughts within our minds which overcome the superior self by usurping its place. In *Splitting Apart* (23), which as a hexagram refers to the takeover of the inferiors, or "evil element" as it is also called, a line reads, "The leg of the bed is split." This refers to the beginning collapse of our serenity, because a shadow of doubt has begun to infiltrate our peace of mind. As a result, our rest, symbolized by the bed, is disturbed. The commentary to this line explains that "those followers of the ruler who remain loyal are destroyed by slander and intrigue." In this case, the followers are the good aspects of our character: patience, willingness to be led, sincerity in following the good, and detachment. Doubt, with its attendant rationales, collapses our perseverance; even the slightest listening to doubt is followed by the inferiors' taking over, demanding us to take aggressive action. This is the essence of splitting apart—leaving the path of correct waiting.

The inferiors vary in the degree of evil and danger they present. Those described as animals often refer to single inferior ideas or habits of mind to which we might be attached. The pheasant mentioned in *The Wanderer* (56) represents a pleasantry—a comfortable but incorrect attitude we could easily give up. "He shoots a pheasant. It drops with the first arrow. In the end this brings both praise and office." In *The Power of the Great* (34) a goat "butts against a hedge and becomes entangled"; this pictures obstinacy, the readiness to push our ideas on others or to continue an action even though we know it to be wrong. "Pigs and fishes" symbolize persons who are intractable and difficult to influence, because their inferiors are the established leaders of their personalities. A cock crowing symbolizes the emptiness of trying to influence people by mere words. Game which must be caught because it "is devastating the fields" symbolizes destructive negative ideas. A hamster hiding things in its nest symbolizes harboring bad habits of mind. "Three flattering foxes" represent ideas we like because they flatter our self-image. A "hawk on a high wall" which must be "forcibly removed" because "he is hardened in his wickedness" represents a powerful negative self-image, such as pride, which obstructs progress; it is so firmly attached to our way of thinking that, like the undisciplined crew of my ship, there is nothing to do but to "kill it."

Action which arises in the toes, calves, thighs, jaws, cheeks, and tongue symbolizes thoughtless action that springs impulsively from hidden negative ideas, faulty traditions, and pacts we have previously made with ourselves. These ideas and pacts are so habitual that they spring into action without our having consciously thought them first.

When we grow up, the inferior ideas become more organized by our emerging self-identity, or ego; they are described in *The Army* (7) as an undisciplined army that can swiftly turn into a mob that is out of hand; in another hexagram they are unreliable men- and maid-servants that can easily turn into criminals and slanderers who are incorribibly obstinate. "Comrades who are envious" become comrades who "no longer heed any warning."

The Inferior Man

When the inferiors are hardened under the leadership of the ego-self-image as an organized response to things, the *I Ching* begins to refer to them as the *inferior man,* instead of *men*, and the "ringleader of disorder," "a tyrant," and "the Commander of Darkness." These organized responses come from fixed sets of defenses such as those that occur when pride, on being injured, hardens into vanity. The inferior man, then, is the accumulated and fixed image of our self, with its train of rights and privileges. In any given situation we already know how a person will behave, because of his set responses. The superior man, too, is firm in his overall principles, but the firmness comes, not from externally added beliefs which are the product of negative experiences but from an inner awareness of the center of himself, and his unwillingness to depart from that center. The images that create the inferior man are drawn from the wish to defend oneself against failure; because they rest on childhood fears, they can only be overcome by a most resolute and determined attitude

43

to be free of them, once we have recognized them as false and destructive. This determination is required because the ego, as a defense mechanism, resists any attempt to displace it; this is to say, it defends its own existence as well as it defends the hiding place of our fears. The superior man that remains when we have shed the inferior man appears to be defenseless, but because he clings to the power of truth, and depends upon the higher forces, he is defended. Because he is free of the dark power, the light power is able to come to his aid. This dependence does not mean that he has "faith," or presumes upon his luck, but that he is resolute against doubt. Through resoluteness, his attitude remains neutral and receptive, and he accepts things as they come.

Various lines in the *I Ching* refer to the quality of resoluteness that is necessary if we are to free ourselves from the inferior man. Pride and vanity are the same hawk on a high wall that must be shot down in the sixth line of *Deliverance* (40). The sixth line of *The Clinging* (30) speaks of "ringleaders" that "must be killed." The followers, or simple inferiors that have been fooled by the rationales of the ringleaders, are to be "spared," which is to say that we need not punish ourselves or indulge feelings of guilt. It is simply enough to recognize that we have been fooled, and to remain resolute against these rationales, as the inferior man tries, through force of habit, to re-insert them into our way of thinking. Through making the effort to free ourselves from these resistant and destructive aspects of our nature, we come to know evil; we understand how powerful the dark force is and are able to be compassionate with the mistakes of others.

The ego is mentioned in *Keeping Still* (52) as that part of our self from which we must become free before we are able to hear suggestions from the inner world. In a state of inner quiet, "the ego with its restlessness, disappears...." In *Dispersion* (57), egotism leads to "separation from all others," causing disunity and alienation. When we concentrate on defining ourselves as different from each other, and cultivate pride in being a certain sort of individual, we begin to build our life around what makes us different. In focusing on our differences, we lose the sense of oneness that unites us with others. Alienation and disunity are contrary to our true nature.

The inferior man, or ego-self-image, arises out of feelings of insufficiency of self. The extent to which this self-image is developed is proportionate to the quantity of self-doubt that we accept as we go along. It arises, as well, from a primitive fear that the Creative may not exist, or, if it does exist, it is not necessarily favorable to our existence, and might even be hostile. Intuitively, we know the hidden implications of such thought processes. Once our true self, or inner eye, is shown an array of doubts by our conscious mind, we may not know what to think, especially if the "proof" is offered by our intellect that other people believe in these doubts, and "shouldn't they know?" If we accept these doubts as possible, or even linger in entertaining them, they gain credibility and soon become accepted. Then the doubts overweigh the intuitive perception, which is thereafter put aside, or imprisoned by the logic of the intellect.

Our first self-doubt may occur when, as infants, arbitrary feeding schedules are arranged for us in the belief that we "don't know when we are hungry," and from the fear that to promptly respond to our needs might "make a monster" of us. We intuitively understand the implications of these doubts about our intrinsic goodness and competence. Later, when our parents think we must "become" a certain type of person, they transmit another of their doubts about our ability to survive without transforming ourselves into something better than what we are. Moreover, in putting the question of survival in purely external terms, they automatically communicate their doubt about the existence of the hidden world and the power of the Creative to help us get along—which partnership, its discovery and fulfillment, is the primary reason for our coming into existence in the first place. Parents do this, of course, because it was done to them.

This double question of insufficiency of self and doubt of the Creative, is experienced as a trap, as being thrust into life as an insufficient person, with no resources and no way out. Our very confidence in life's having a purpose is placed in jeopardy. This uncertainty is experienced as anxiety, and a hollow feeling in the center of the chest, as if we have been directly wounded at the center of our being. (Nearly everyone can recall having felt this way about life at one time or another.) This feeling of entrapment, so long as it is there, and even though it is only subjectively experienced, demands that we do something about it. An equally strong positive feeling is needed in compensation, to relieve the pressure of the anxiety. This is our first real knowledge of loneliness and insecurity; it may occur in varying degrees and at varying times during our lives.

Obviously, this negative feeling starts in small ways; more self-doubt about the worth of their being is generally inculated into the minds of little girls than into the minds of little boys; but doubt is inculated into little boys' minds if they do not measure up to the prescribed image of what little boys must be. Even those who do "measure up" have doubt because they know they are conforming to a false image—an image to which they sacrifice their feelings of self-worth, in exchange for acceptance.

All of us have doubts about ourselves. No matter how small, these doubts are problems from the point of view of the *I Ching*. In the hexagram *Break-through/Resoluteness* (43), it is mentioned that "even if only one inferior man is occupying a ruling position in a city, he is able to oppress superior men. Even a single passion still lurking in the heart has power to obscure reason. Passion and reason cannot exist side by side—therefore fight without quarter is necessary if the good is to prevail." As long as the negative feeling exists within us, we are put in the same position as the drug addict trying to find a "fix," only we seek one that will free us from that feeling in our chest. Not until we dismantle, through self-development, all the rationales of disbelief that we have accepted over the years do we become truly enough by simply being ourselves. Then we become liberated from the entraping mechanisms upon which we have learned to rely. This is the meaning of enlightenment.

Meanwhile, during the normal course of life, we are in search of "solutions" to this negative pressure that will keep the gnawing anxiety at bay. When we first feel this insufficiency of self and entrapment by life, the emotionalism of our inferiors is extreme—hysterical, in fact, demanding that something "be done." The logic of the inferiors goes like this: "Indeed, if it is true that there is no one to help us but ourselves, we must choose qualities of being that will preserve us from harm. Being free of harm, we can then make this purposeless life as good as possible." From this time on, the inferiors are in charge of what we come to think of as our self, and our self-interest. They accumulate aspects modelled on one or another person who appears to be succeeding; if, in adopting a new characteristic, we find that the hollow feeling is less frequent, or temporarily gone, we accept that quality as part of our self-image. Piece by piece, the inferiors construct a personality that defends this "vulnerable spot" from the proddings and challenges of others. Strangely enough, everyone knows the vulnerable spot in others. Most of us don't prod it in each other because we don't want ours prodded in return; but doing so gives some people a feeling of superiority—that positive charge that helps them compensate for their own feelings of inferiority.

From the time we construct our "external personality" or mask with which to deal with the world, we address the external world as the only real issue of life. The validity and reality of our real self is put aside, along with the validity and reality of the Creative, and the hidden world. This is not always a total thing because we construct protections only in those areas in which we have doubt and fear; other areas exist which we take for granted as being harmless. But in whatever area we have constructed these protections, the power of the Creative does not enter; the light force never intermingles with the dark force.

Having composed our new personality, a phenomenon takes place. The playwright, Pirandello, observed that when he began to create a character, it tried to "take over" and exercise its own demands. It would no longer come in and go out on cue. This made it difficult to give the play dramatic structure, for each character protested against fitting into a secondary position; each wanted to tell his own story exclusively and dominate the play. This phenomenon caused Pirandello to write *Six Characters in Search of an Author,* in which, one by one, each of six characters entered an empty stage and demanded to see the director and have his story told. It is the same when we create a self-image. The ego emerges and takes over, demanding that the entire personality fulfill the role it has decided to play. The true self cannot do this; thereafter it remains a prisoner of the ego, inherently in conflict with it, but helpless to counteract it until such time

47

as, by reason of adversity and shock, the ego is no longer able to protect the inferiors; then, they, in dismay, look about once more for other solutions. During such times, we witness the temporary collapse of the ego-self-image—a momentous time. Like the Wicked Witch of the West in *Wizard of Oz*, it simply disintegrates into dust.

As an image, the ego is only a false self, separate and distinct. In meditation experiences our real self, or inner eye, sees the ego as a separate entity; at its worst, it appears in animal or demonic form as a dragon, a bear, or a snake, or a similarly fearful image. Often the ego appears as something fearful, being the creature of our fear and doubt, but it may also be in a variety of human forms—ourselves projected as someone glamorous, witty, or exciting when we are in an enthusiastic mood, or as a miserable hulk—incapable of achieving anything, dull and uninteresting, and an outright failure, when we are in a dark, self-flagellating mood. The ego has achieved such dominance of our personality only because our real self has unwittingly acquiesced in the fundamental doubt of self and doubt of the Creative put forward by the gullible and hysterical inferiors.

In its separate existence, the ego-self-image retains the power of the dark force, and is self-perpetuating as well as self-protecting. Our fear of meditation is caused by the warnings and threats given off by our ego, which knows that through meditation, it may be unmasked and stripped of its powers. Its threats are no more harmful than were those of the Wizard of Oz, when stripped of his fearful machinery. The dragons of fear are but paper dragons, and their existence depends on hiding this fact from us.

The following account of a meditation experience gives an example of my dealing with one aspect of my own ego-self-image. I saw two dots of light—so small, yet distinct, that it was hard to imagine what they might be, except that they were spaced apart about the distance that eyes might be spaced. Nevertheless, I could not recall ever having seen any eyes so small as these two dots. Then I noticed that the dots seemed to be surrounded by larger, dark, glazed-over orbs, so that the whole appeared to be sleepy eyes. Immediately I realized that that was what they were—sleepy eyes! Then this image was replaced by another, that of puffs of smoke floating upward, such as those given off by a coal-fired railroad engine that is resting on a track. I would have thought the puffs were coming from just such an engine, were it not for a reddish glow that shone upwards onto the bottom of the puffs. I also noted that the puffs were timed to the beat of my own heart.

Then I saw that those puffs were coming from a sleeping, or nearly asleep dragon, whose eyes were barely open—only enough for the tiny dots of light to be seen. The fire outlining the puffs of smoke was simply part of its acrid nature. I no sooner noted that it was half-awake than I found myself with a bow and arrow. It was obvious that I was meant to shoot it, which I did at once, aiming straight at its eye; the shot went into its brain and killed it. Then I cut it into pieces with a sword (which magically appeared in my hand), and offered it as a sacrifice to the higher power, which, I realized, thought of it as a delicacy. It was immediately dispatched.

Next, the chamber in which all this took place came into focus. It was an odd, tunnel-like room that reminded me of the chamber of a heart, except that it was obvious that this was a very large room. Then I realized that because the puffs of smoke were timed to my heartbeat, this dragon was really inside my heart! Moreover, I noted that the puffs had the same sound I make when, inside myself, I self-righteously say, "Harumph!" in response to seeing other people's inferior behavior. Clearly, this was the dragon of my own self-righteousness! During the week that preceded this meditation I had had several experiences in which I felt especially strong inner "Harumphs!" I began to realize that the dragon's beady eyes were like my own when I stared at people with incredulity at their behavior or thinking. Obviously, my gaze had been fastened on them, at least inwardly, and was narrowed down to the most narrow hardness of feeling as I mentally reproached them for their cupidity, their stupidity, their infidelity to their real natures, and so on.

As long as the ego predominates, it is aware that it cannot replace our real self; it knows that it can never exist except as an image, or have the potential immortality of the real self, yet it wants to be us, and to have the immortality if it can somehow figure out how to attain it. It tries to deny everything that would deny its existence, therefore it constantly demonstrates before our real self that it is the best-equipped leader of the self. This is a kind of parade before our inner mirror: "I'm okay, am I not?" "I'm doing a fine job, aren't I?" "Boy, I really impressed them... see that!" This monologue is carried on as if our ego is on a stage before our real self as the voiceless audience, which it is always trying to impress and convince. The ego also spends a good deal of energy trying to verify its existence by acquiring recognition in other people's eyes. "Yes, you do exist," we seem to say when we give someone the feedback they require.

This ego-self is the ringleader of self-deceptions. It looks ahead to anticipate events; it looks behind to see if it can pat itself on the back for things accomplished; it fancies that it is responsible for every good thing that happens to us and is never responsible for anything bad that happens to us. It is full of self-praise, bravado, and, on certain occasions, exuberant enthusiasm. Just as often, however, it engages in dark-seeing—taking a dim view of people and events. "Prices are too high; taxes are too high; the system is out to get us; Fate is hostile," etc. Thus, the inferiors, under the dominance of the dark-seeing ego, whine and despair when the outlook is dark and are enthusiastic and gleeful when things look good. When things are going well, the ego tends to assume that good times will last forever, therefore indulges in arrogant presumptions. When things are not going well, it tends to assume that hard times are going to continue on and on, with no end in sight. It alternates between hope and despair. It is no wonder that the *I Ching* refers to it as the "Lord of Darkness."

Once dispersed, the ego re-emerges in a seductive manner. The hexagram *Coming to Meet* (44) describes its entrance in detail. The ego re-enters as a hardly noticeable, slightly negative mood. Soon, however, the whining, self-pitying voice of the inferiors begins, upon begin subjected to the negativism of doubt. At first, the ego's rationale seems weak or harmless and we mistakenly think we might listen to its entreaties without getting drawn in. But once we entertain what it says, it suddenly commands us to act and change things; "either cut bad things off or not!" If we observe someone else being less than true to himself, our ego demands that we comdemn him at once. When it has attained full strength, the ego is blatently obstinate, proud, defensive, and factional; it thinks of itself as decisive, and resists self-development and discipline; it calculates and contrives, is restless and ambitious; it indulges glory-seeking and is one-track minded, but in its ambitiousness, it will try to do a hundred things at once; it knows no limits: it exuberantly admires, passionately hates, indulges petty likes and dislikes, pretends, and is anxious that others do their share; it looks up to heaven for protection while engaging in wrong acts; it weighs and measures everything and constantly looks in its inner mirror to see how it is succeeding; it seeks the glory of the high road and disdains the quiet patience of the low road; it is envious, vindictive, and impatient; it constantly sees all these negative qualities in others, but does not see them in itself. In the clinches, and during shock, it disappears, for it is a true coward, as well as a bully. (For this reason, the *I Ching* sometimes teaches by use of shock—that is, shocking events in our external life are explained as being the only way to de-structure particularly rigid ideas.) The ego is easily bored, hence seeks excitement and sensation. This desire for excitement also stems from an inordinate curiosity. It never seeks true learning but desires only to see how it can use knowledge to further its own image. It is sleepy-minded and goes to sleep when we keep still. For this reason, "keeping still," or meditating, is important in gaining control over our ego. Its strength rests on all the secret fears we have stored within; as fear, it has a thousand disguises, but when we begin to know them we are able to be decisive against them and gain power over them.

As an organized response to events, the ego prevents our being helped and led by the higher power, for we can only receive such help if we remain unstructured in our thinking. The voices of the inferiors and the ego become so insistent, they so clutter our inner space, that we are unable to hear the Creative within. The genie is blocked off. The inner eye is forced to see the parade of images put before it by the inferiors. The ego's organized pacts to do or not do things "The next time something happens" so programs our life that natural spontaneity, by which the perfect response to situations is made possible, is lost. The risks of change are so carefully channeled and neutralized by defense-mechanisms that we become barricaded against life and are no longer able to understand its meaning.

The fundamental conflict posed by the rise of the inferior man sooner or later comes to a head. As the sixth line of *The Receptive* (2) puts it, "Dragons fight in the meadow." "The dragon, symbol of heaven, comes to fight the false dragon that symbolizes the inflation of the earth principle." In this battle the dark power is inevitably overthrown. This life or death conflict is predestined by elements in our attitude, for as long as we choose to follow a false path, its dead-end is sure to become visible and finally stand squarely before us as that obstruction the *I Ching* calls "Fate."

While our immediate response to this obstruction is to think that we have no alternatives, we are really at an important cross-roads; one of these roads leads to developing the higher aspects of our nature, the other to evading the issue by seeking a new set of defenses in a new self-image. Intuitively we know that the only way we may fulfill our life's goal is by developing our higher nature. Our inferiors also seek these higher goals, but they have not the means to find the way. The idea that they can lead our personality to this higher success is one of the great delusions of the ego-self-image. Only that which is in harmony with the Cosmic Law is allowed; there are no short-cuts, despite the enthusiasm with which our ego proclaims, from time to time, that it has "found the way." Whether we respond to this opportunity to follow the inner path of spiritual development, using the *I Ching* as a lantern to find the way, is entirely up to us. As the ancient Greeks would have put it, the road lies through the underworld, and requires that we pass Cerberus, the three-headed dog (our ego) which guards the entrance, and slay the dragons of fear that guard the inner treasure.

Self-development

Fate, in the *I Ching,* means two things: first, it is that of destiny—our personal Tao to fulfill the higher image of us that is stored in the mind of the Deity. To fail this destiny, as in avoiding it, is to engage Fate in its second meaning—as an obstruction. This obstruction is found at the end of each wrong road we follow. Fate stands squarely across every path charted and managed by our ego-self-image. It is only a matter of time before we meet it. Fate is not antagonistic or vindictive; it is there to teach us, in an impersonal way, that the goal may not be gained through false means. The Sage and Fate work as a pair, the Sage to guide and help, Fate as the dilemma that forces us to seek help. Fate, therefore, is both our innate destiny and the obstruction that comes from avoiding that destiny.

Fate, as an obstruction, is a door that can be unlocked, but only by the proper key—which is a correct attitude. Upon correcting our attitude we find that our situation improves; but if we then become careless and revert to the incorrect attitude, the door closes once more. Fate, as an obstruction, seems to match us move for move once we have come to this impasse; where we once seemed to be free to err, with no penalty attached, now we have to immediately pay for every mistake; it is as if we have had our credit card taken away. Our way around the obstruction must conform to Cosmic Laws, as the commentary to the third line in *Difficulty at the Beginning* (3) states: "If a man tries to hunt in a strange forest and has no guide, he loses his way. When he finds himself in difficulties he must not try to steal out of them unthinkingly and without guidance. Fate cannot be duped; premature effort, without the necessary guidance, ends in failure and disgrace. Therefore the superior man, discerning the seeds of coming events, prefers to renounce a wish rather than to provoke failure and humiliation by trying to force its fulfillment."

On attempting to find ways around this obstruction, it becomes clear that our ego (as wit and brilliance) is unable to deal with it. The shock of failing in our assault upon the problem has the dual effect of turning the ego to rout, because, in all states of shock, the humbling of the inferiors causes their ego creature to fail, or disappear—at least for the time being. With the ego temporarily gone, the inferiors suddenly have no solutions. At this point we have the opportunity to reestablish the leadership of the superior self. However, this is also a point in time in which the superior self is undeveloped and out of practice in leading the personality; it has forgotten quiet acquiescence; the ability to persevere has to be reawakened. Meanwhile, the inferiors are only momentarily

53

submissive; they readily regain confidence when the situation improves in the slightest degree, and remain docile only so long as the external situation keeps them under pressure. At this point we may well get the fifth line of *Enthusiasm* (16), which says, "Persistently ill, and still does not die." The commentary adds, "A man is under constant pressure... however, this pressure has its advantages—it prevents him from consuming his powers in empty enthusiasm. Thus, constant pressure can actually serve to keep him alive." This is also to say that, in a weakened state of will, we cannot afford the luxury of more false moves. During this time we tend to feel a see-sawing effect as the ego is first suppressed by the humbling of the inferiors, then re-emerges as the seriousness of the external situation eases. Very often we are suffering from ill health because of the exhaustive effect of internal conflict and the oppressiveness of doubt. Our life's limited quantity of energy has seemingly dried up. The hexagram *Oppression (Exhaustion)* (47) compares our situation to that of a lake which has dried up.

Another deficiency of our situation comes from the attachment that our emotional body has to our ego-self-image; this causes the inferiors to perceive their welfare as dependent upon the well-being of the ego; therefore, as the fate of the ego rises and falls, their sense of well-being rises and falls accordingly. That they are dependent upon the ego is a misconception on their part; they are as yet unaware that their well-being really depends upon their being detached from the ego, and that they can safely let it go. A part of the ego's hold on them comes from its having convinced them that "without experiencing emotional heights, you aren't alive." It has taught them to live for and anticipate these highs. As a consequence, they do not remember—or have confidence in the fact—that true joy is found in a serene and quiet soul. It is necessary, in this dilemma, to detach the way we feel (our emotional body) from our self-image. While this is difficult, it is not impossible, but it does require that we allow ourselves to be led by the higher power which, alone, knows the way.

In the work of self-renewal, or return to our original self, we may not simulate correct attitudes by adopting them, as one adopts a religion or belief, or a passionate feeling. Correct attitudes are true to our nature and cannot be added, as in saying "Now I'll do this," or "I will agree to that." In these cases our intellect says what we may do, and tries to memorize an approach so that it may remain in control. There are no sets of rules we may look up in the book that tells us what to do in each different situation. If anything, the rule is that we may not know anything in advance; we may know only what our inner moral guidelines are, and when each situation arrives we must refer back to these to see how we may fit into the situation, and with a sincere mind, seek clarity to find the correct action. To attain clarity, we must subtract the intellect and come to a state of inner quiet and acceptance. Clarity comes as a clear perception and penetrating realization, and always coincides with the realization that we have been prohibited from following this natural way precisely because of those attitudes we have taken on. We also realize that because the force of habit is strong, our new clarity must be vigorously maintained if the inferior ideas are not to re-establish themselves.

Similarly, we cannot find the correct way by intellectually analyzing what it is. For example, in reading a book such as this about the *I Ching,* our ego may assume it knows what the *I Ching* is about, and that all there is to growing is to conceptualize its ideas. This is not possible, for every lesson must be internalized through experience in a one-to-one relationship with the Sage. The Sage, not our intellect, must be the teacher.

In working with the *I Ching,* we gradually ferret our hidden fears from their hiding places. The progress is necessarily slow and piecemeal, so that the fears are diminished in strength. When they are in a greatly weakened state, we face them at their point of origin; our strength is in place and we have the help we need from the hidden world to eradicate them. In this manner they are unable to attack from behind while we face them in front. Because these fears are stored as images which have the demonic form of our childish imagination (for indeed, they are derived from our childhood), to find and deal with them is a serious business, one which requires amassing the strength of character (weaponry) that only the Sage knows how to help us attain. The progress must be slow and steady. Our sincerity, our asking for help, brings the help we need. The qualities of character that become our most powerful weapons are those of acceptance and modesty.

Besides the hazards presented by the demonic fears within, we can hardly have anticipated that our ego will join the effort to make progress, once it sees we are determined to follow the path of self-development. This involvement of our ego becomes obvious when we find ourselves exasperated at "how long it takes" to make visible progress. Our ego is at work looking forward to the goal, counting the time for us; it tallies every effort and measures how far away it still remains and reminds us at every moment how difficult and "probably impossible" it is to do things this way. The Sage does not become involved with our ego's hopes for reward, therefore, progress halts. Self-development is not something we can strive for, but something that happens within through slow, patient work on ourselves.

Through consulting the *I Ching* daily, we learn how to be led and defended by the Creative Power. We learn to apprehend the moods of the encroaching inferiors and to discipline them to be led and to wait, without knowing what is going to happen, and to do it patiently and willingly instead of anxiously and grudgingly. In order to achieve anything, the *I Ching* emphasizes the necessity of gaining the inner assent of our inferiors; if our effort involves relating to someone else, we must gain the assent of their inferiors. This means that our inferiors must sometimes endure privations and work in a menial and unnoticed position; they learn to endure being misunderstood, with patience, and to sacrifice feelings of anger and frustration, for the good of the situation. They learn, in following this path, to be devoted to good for its own sake, without demanding that others think of them as good. This is to be "modest about their modesty." In eastern religions such as Buddhism and Zen, training emphasizes the discipline and obedience of the inferiors. One sect or another practices enduring hunger or pain. The Sage, of course, requires no such exercises, but the work of self-development through the *I Ching* is the same—to bring the inferiors to obedience and coordination. In *The Army* (7), they are spoken of as "troops" which must be disciplined and obedient if the trials and challenges we meet are to be conquered. Their willingness to undergo privations for the sake of the greater goals of the personality makes it possible to accomplish great feats.

The work of disciplining our inferiors has several objects. The first and most important object is that of attaining clarity, for when we see clearly what to do, it is easy to do it. To see with clarity requires that we train our inferiors to keep still, and leave our mental space open. Next we train our inferiors to keep disengaged upon seeing other people's inferiors; we recognize the presence of evil, but refrain from allowing our inferiors to brand evil by saying what the evil "is." We keep the evil at arm's length and in our peripheral view only, so as not to lose our own purity of mind. Likewise, our inferiors are trained to resist the temptation to vie with others, to engage in smart exchanges or arguments, and to parade and demonstrate our personality. These temptations, if not resisted, allow our ego to take over. Next we train our inferiors to disengage from situations in which they have already become involved; in doing this we require them to disperse feelings of anger and alienation, and to sacrifice their accustomed assertion of rights. Finally, we train the inferiors to respond to patience and to persevere; this we do by teaching them to cling to the idea of the "great man" within everyone, even when the worst aspects of that person are dominating them. We also train our inferiors to be on guard against succumbing to self-flattery when success begins to result from our growth and development.

By controlling the inferiors, by strengthening the good aspects of our personality, we rescue ourself. By rescuing oneself, we fulfill a part of the Creative design to rescue the higher nature of others, for, by following the path of the good, we win the hearts of others to follow it. What we are penetrates through to others in a re-vitalizing way, and they see, from their own insight, the power of the good. Our influence on others is not through intentional effort. Being devoted to our path, we do not parade it before others. If the injustices of others requires us to endure being misunderstood, our perseverance is not something they see, for we demonstrate nothing; we do not try to impress them with the truth of the situation, but depend on truth's penetrating power. Similarly, we do not proselytize our way of life; it is consistent with respect for the dignity of others to allow them to find their own way. To take advantage of every opportunity to explain our way of life is to be too ambitious and conscious in our effort. Certainly, to press ourselves upon others is to have ego-involvement in our way of making progress. The *I Ching* calls this "using power." At the same time, if people ask for help and are open to our views, it is our duty to "meet them halfway," and to respond sincerely. The correct way of making progress is by depending upon the pentrating effect of a good example—the impact of our whole way of life.

We are able to help others when we respond spontaneously to the "moments of opportunity" that occur. These moments comprise short lengths of time when people are open and receptive to our views. Then we have a chance to explain what is appropriate to that moment and what applies in the most essential way. As long as we strictly adhere to what is appropriate and essential, and keep our attitude in balance, the moment stays open. But when we begin to enjoy our influence, or become expansive, or begin to use what we say to promote ourselves, the moment closes, because our ego has entered the scene. If we then fail to disengage, the good effect of our work is reversed; if we press on, we "throw ourselves away." This loss of inner independence is humiliating, because, due to the pressure of our inferiors, we have willfully given up a position of strength for one of weakness; the consequent damage to our personality is called "darkening of the light."

Self-development makes us sensitive to the opening and the waning of these moments of opportunity. This sensitivity is respectful of the dignity of others and gives them the space they need to find the correct way. Throughout these cycles of influence we hold to the idea of their "great man" within. In not doubting their ability to find the way, we gradually win their inner assent to follow their own superior natures. This is how the Sage helps us, and it is how we help others.

In his contact with others, the follower of the Sage does not defend his point-of-view. To explain is one thing; to defend is to become engaged with the other person's ego. It is better to go on one's way and be misunderstood, as this is no deterrence to progress. Paradoxically, we must allow a misunderstanding of our views as a step in the process of understanding. In such a manner do we alternately misunderstand and understand the way of the Sage. While we do not encourage misunderstandings, we are not dismayed or alarmed when they happen. Again, we do not intend any effect, but we relate to each misunderstanding and obstruction patiently, knowing that time is the vehicle by which they will be resolved.

It is part of the greatness of truth that it is displayed ironically. The Sage, we might say, likes irony. Or, we might say that the presence of both dark and light are necessary to seeing. Just when we are sure that a happening was disastrous, we begin to find that it has been accompanied by hidden benefits; indeed, bad luck has only been a disguise for good luck; when we think we have been abandoned and left alone, help has been arising from a new quarter all the while. This is the way of the Sage. Understanding and help provide the denouement. Truth, which we thought to be grim, is all light and relief.

This irony is the message of the hexagram *Opposition* (38), which means "misunderstanding." We misunderstand the meaning of life and the meaning of death when we think that God and Fate are hostile. When we think that life is unfair, as when someone dies and is "taken from us," this mistrust of God and Fate causes us internal conflict; it is against our nature to rail at God. When we decide that death, as something we don't understand, is a negative thing, we shut ourselves off from any higher understanding of it. When we are in this hostile mood, we tend to get lines such as the third in *Opposition*: "Isolated through opposition, one meets a like-minded man with whom one can associate in good faith. Despite the danger, no blame." The commentary explains that if the person can let go of his mistrust, the dangers of isolation will be overcome. The sixth line also refers to isolation "due to misunderstanding." This misunderstanding causes a person to "misjudge his best friends, taking them to be unclean as a dirty pig and as dangerous as a wagon full of devils." In time, it says, he will see his mistake and overcome the danger of seeing things in the wrong light. Misunderstandings are caused from misreading the meaning of events. The second line of *The Clinging* (30) refers to truth as having a "yellow" rather than a white, glaring light. Truth is moderate and soft, not harsh and unpleasant. We often over-read the hexagrams because of this tendency to see things in their extreme. We do this because our inferiors (or our ego) are seeing things for us; they are acting as our sentinels, interpreting events according to standards that have nothing to do with the higher truth.

The effect of self-development is to moderate the way we see things through dismissing our inferiors and displacing our ego as the interpreters. We take things seriously, but not too seriously; we attain the middle road, or as Confucius put it, the mean. We work at our development steadily and patiently rather than with fervour. Although we are conscientious in trying to keep our attitudes correct, we do not despair when we make mistakes; if we slide backwards, we accept the setback and start again from this new place without attaching ourselves to the idea of failure. We are conscientious to have the correct effect on other people, but we also do not attach ourselves to the impressions we make or fail to make on them. We let go of past errors, omissions and regrets; they only inhibit inner power and engage fear and pride. We contemplate the past only to recognize and correct our errors, but we don't dwell on them, rather, we forgive ourselves for our shortcomings. It is enough to be resolved to try to do the correct thing in the future. It is self-flattery to think that life hangs on our remembered mistakes; through self-development their importance and their bad effects disappear.

The meaning of acceptance so frequently counseled in the *I Ching* is interpreted in the context of the mean. Acceptance is not "Well, that's the way it is," when something happens we don't understand; in deciding a thing is either negative or positive, we go too far; acceptance is to leave the event unstructued by not deciding what it is. This sort of open-mindedness enables the higher truth to come through. Acceptance means to flow with the situation unresistingly, which requires keeping the fearful, doubting voices of our inferiors stilled; we refuse to look at their pointing to all the evidence they see as either dim or hopeful. Acceptance is close to the idea of modesty in that it requires a certain resoluteness on our part to be decisive against our inferiors; but resoluteness must not lead to being so bent on defeating our inferiors that we can no longer hear from within. Everything cannot be achieved through effort. Part of being moderate is that we accept those areas in which we need help from the higher scource. We are not capable, all by ourselves, of holding our inferiors in check on every occasion, yet in putting forth the effort to do so, and in asking for help, we get the help of the Sage to overcome their influence and "bring things to completion."

The entire business of the *I Ching* is to re-affirm our knowledge of God as the higher power, not only as a vague, intuitive knowledge, but as a conscious, practical, intimate, everyday knowledge. This means that we materalize the reality of God out of the mists of our unconscious into the full reality of consciousness. We may know intuitively that someone we love is unfaithful to us, but when this knowledge surfaces by evidence into consciousness, it produces such a shock that it is hard to understand the difference between these two sorts of knowing. We may know someone is dying of cancer for a long time, but the fact of their death produces an unexpectedly strong emotional response. How do we explain this? When the ego leads our personality, the conscious mind disbelieves what we intuitively know; moreover, the ego insists that conscious reality is the only reality—in this case it does not want to believe that death exists. When death, the objective fact happens, the conscious mind is unprepared, and the ego disappears in the ensuing shock. One's knowledge of God is similar. In the beginning of self-development we know about God intuitively and theoretically; we may have occasionally experienced the higher power, but afterwards we have rationalized the experience as some quirk of our imagination; soon, it seems it never happened at all. Our intuition of God, through this process, has become dimmed. Through self-development, however, we come to experience the reality of God as an everyday fact of life. We experience God directly, not only in small ways, but in big ways, so that even the smallest errors of perception are swept away. This daily relating to the higher power gradually erases every particle of doubt.

Eradicating doubt in its least visible forms and at its most germinal inceptions is our daily work. We cannot elevate ourselves over doubt by deciding to have faith, whereby doubt is really still there. To get around the half-believing, half-doubting state that comes from experiencing God sporadically, we may consciously decide to believe in God without dealing with the residual elements of doubt which we carry in our everyday attitudes. By deciding to have faith, we simply cover these doubts up. Then we defend our faith from the intuitive awareness that we have not yet conquered our doubts. Faith, in this manifestation, is another trick played upon us by our ego, and another defense against the unknown. Only by the most determined search can we find and eradicate all doubt within ourselves. Meanwhile, we are helped in our effort by God as the unknown, invisible, unnameable but viable and constantly felt force. Our new state is not faith or belief, or doubt or disbelief, but an unrational awareness.

As followers of the Sage we may not possess the truth. It is not ours to have or to put upon others. We may each help the other, but everyone must find truth within himself. We are always in a process of searching for the truth; it comes when it will, and that is that. It comes freely and fully as long as we place ourselves in proximity to it, but if we pretend that we have special access to it, or if we parade the honors we earn by our work, we soon find the well of truth inaccessible. The wise person is content to be a seeker, never forgetting that everything he earns through perseverance and devotion is, nevertheless, a gift. It is the result of "coming to meet halfway."

The well of wisdom is available to all who come. Not infrequently we hear children and uneducated people say wise things; innocent and honest hearts are a ready conduit for the profound. If we are attuned to it, the Sage speaks to us in a thousand ways.

4.

The Sage-Student Relationship

Because the voice which speaks through the *I Ching* has a certain personality, the Sage shall hereafter be referred to more conveniently as "he." However, this does not mean "he" as masculine. "He" is simply an entity with specific values and ways of dealing with our attitudes and problems. These and the following pages discuss in detail the way this personality works.

For example, as it was mentioned before, the Sage tends to address only our questions of greatest inner concern, whether we phrase them or not, ignoring superficial and secondary questions. This does not mean the Sage will not answer secondary questions, but that more basic questions must be answered before secondary questions can be addressed. The Sage builds our understanding from the ground up, putting everything in its appropriate place and relationship in order that we may see things from the Cosmic Viewpoint. The Sage wastes no time on non-essentials or trivialities.

It was also mentioned before that when we consult the *I Ching* more than once at a sitting, we find the successive hexagrams elaborate and clarify the message of the first hexagram. This, too, is in keeping with the teaching methods of the Sage. It is the tendency of our inferiors to flit like birds from tree to tree in the hopes of scouting out the problem from above without getting involved in its details. The Sage, if anything, belabors the question and will not budge from it until we have understood the reply in all its ramifications. Eventually, we begin to see that this is a very tolerant way of dealing with our inferiors, and, on the point of understanding this, we are likely to receive the following line from *Approach* (19): "A Sage who has put the world behind him and who in spirit has already withdrawn from life may, under certain circumstances, decide to return once more to the here and now

63

to approach other men. This means great good fortune for the men whom he teaches and helps. And for him this great-hearted humbling of himself is blameless." A line in *Youthful Folly* (4) further describes this patient, plodding way the Sage teaches us: "... character is developed by thoroughness that skips nothing but, like water, gradually and steadily fills up all gaps and so flows onward."

On first approaching the Sage, our inferior and superior aspects of character are intermingled and disorganized; our knowledge of the affairs of the inner world are virtually non-existent. This state is called "standstill," as the time before self-development. Thereafter, when we get the hexagram *Standstill* (12), it is often in regard to our having fallen back into the habits of mind and patterns of reaction we relied on before we undertook self-development. This state is also called "youthful folly"—a condition of ignorance that, from the view of the Sage, is not a disgrace; after all, we cannot be expected to know about the inner world before we have been guided through it. Thus in *Youthful Folly* it is said, "In the time of youth, folly is not an evil. One may succeed in spite of it, provided one finds an experienced teacher and has the right attitude toward him." In being aware that he needs to know, the student has the necessary modesty to learn; if he then attains "a perseverance that never slackens until the points are mastered one by one...," a "real success is sure to follow."

The method of teaching is to alternate the application of discipline and help with leaving the student free to apply his new knowledge without help. The student invariably fails once or twice, but by being determined to go on, in spite of his failures, he succeeds and masters each lesson. All this is subjectively experienced. In a typical lesson we are confronted with a situation that places us squarely before the problem to be mastered; our first response is traditional and unthinking; only afterwards do we see that we were meant to deal with it differently. Then the same problem occurs again; this time we are more aware, however, our inferiors resist being led and we are not resolute enough, consequently we fail this test as well; the third time we are fully ready; our determination and modesty win the help of the Sage so that the problem is solved. The discipline mentioned above is the pressure put on us by our circumstances (Fate) to correct our way of life. As we correct each faulty attitude we are relieved from a portion of this pressure. At other times when this discipline, or feeling of pressure, is released, all our problems seem to clear away and we begin to experience the euphoria of "life as normal." It is just at this point, however, that we need to be careful, otherwise we begin to think our training has ended and all we need to do hereafter is to enjoy the rewards of our hard work. We fail to realize that the pressure has been removed for a purpose. As the first line in *Youthful Folly* puts it, "discipline should not degenerate into drill." Occasionally, "the fetters" are "removed." The fifth line in *Waiting* (5) also refers to this: "Even in the midst of danger there come intervals of peace when things go relatively well. If we possess enough inner strength, we shall take advantage of these intervals to fortify ourselves for renewed struggle. We must know how to enjoy the moment without being deflected from the goal, for perseverance is needed to remain victorious." The line further explains that "... it is not possible to achieve everything all at once. The height of wisdom is to allow people enough recreation to quicken pleasure in their work until the task is completed." Soon enough, the moments of respite from the pressure and danger end, and our work continues. Through allowing ourselves to be led through such danger and adversity, we develop strength of character, and learn to trust the wisdom and protection given us by the Sage.

In being taught in this manner over a period of years, we discover that the Sage has followed what modern teachers would call a "lesson plan." During the first several years we are mainly concerned with the details of our relationship with the Sage, and the way he deals with our various moods and attitudes.

The Sage teaches all lessons by suggestion. This requires that we develop an open mind. The more structured our thinking, the more difficult it is for us to learn. If we rigidly try to make the answers conform to the literal language of the *I Ching,* we will not understand it, for the images are meant to be taken as analogies. In trying to see each hexagram as a detailed reply to our verbalized question, we miss the fact that it speaks on its own terms, with its own values, to the unspoken inner question we carry with us. The answers have to penetrate through on an inner level, coming to us intuitively. The Sage completely ignores our logical process.

Although we consult the Sage daily, a lesson may require an entire week to complete. As the new lesson begins, we may get the hexagram *Difficulty at the Beginning* (3) which signals that we are being given a new problem. On being confronted with the problem, we often feel unsettled and experience a sense of urgency to find a solution. However, this hexagram warns us not to accept any solutions that suddenly come to mind. By waiting patiently, the correct idea begins to appear. Later, this idea develops into a clear insight as to what attitude we must take to resolve the problem. Often the problem is resolved by simply dispersing inner doubt. Learning to wait in the correct attitude was the whole point of the lesson. Upon perceiving the meaning of the lesson we might get the hexagram *The Gentle (Penetrating)* (57), which means that the correct idea is penetrating our consciousness. The Sage, in effect, is confirming that we have understood correctly.

This kind of slow self-development is described in the hexagram *Development* (53) as being so slow as to be almost imperceptible, but because it is fundamental, touching upon the roots of the problems, its effects are far-reaching and permanent.

This method of teaching by specific external problems is similar to the Zen *coan,* or puzzle, except that our life's problems are the puzzles. One sometimes has the impression that the Sage, in presenting these puzzles to us, has a wry sense of humor, for strive as we do to see a complex meaning in them, they are always surprisingly simple.

The Sage teaches us by a variety of means. Sometimes our readings are clear and obvious; at other times we are meant to digest a series of images without understanding them; the perception breaks through later. On occasions, the message may have nothing to do with the hexagram given; for example, the following question was put to the *I Ching,* using the yarrow stalk method of consulting it: "Does it make any difference whether one uses yarrow stalks or pennies?" An incomprehensible answer followed. The next day the same question was asked, using pennies. Exactly the same hexagram and changing line was received, as if to say, it does not matter which method we use. Because such a variety of means are used to communicate with us, we learn not to presume what the Sage is going to do or say, but to keep our minds open, alert, and unstructured.

Occasionally the Sage ignores all questions to prepare us for an imminently shocking situation. We later realize that we were being given essential help to meet a difficult time. Such a situation happened when a group of friends met weekly to discuss the *I Ching*. It was their regular practice to cast a "group hexagram;" in such cases one of those present usually recognized the hexagram as speaking particularly to them. This time no one felt that the hexagram, *The Taming Power of the Great* (26) with its accompanying line, "He attains the way of heaven, success," pertained to them. As those present sat pondering the matter silently, the telephone rang. The father of a woman at the meeting had just been found dead before his television set. Later that evening, the woman said, she realized the line had been for her benefit. Its meaning had become clear during her grief, and had brought her a profound sense of peace.

A hexagram may call for action. If we assume this means doing something, the next hexagram will warn us from that path. It is difficult to know what action is called for unless we construct several more hexagrams and allow the Sage to make his meaning clear. We are not yet aware that in *I Ching* terms, action almost always refers to deciding not to do something, or being decisive against our inferiors which clamor to take the action they deem best. The action called for in the hexagram *Limitation* (60) is to find the appropriate limits of action. To take action indicated by the hexagram *Retreat* (33) is to retreat from the temptation to engage in conflict with others, or with ourselves. External action is not always incorrect, but whenever we are emotionally engaged, correct action is impossible. True objectivity leads to a just and correct response, one that will not engage inferior aspects in another person's character. To obtain that objectivity, the hexagrams counsel disengagement. The sort of disengagement indicated in the hexagrams may be to retreat from a "dim view" of others, or from feelings of resistance to what is happening to us. This method of not resisting events, of rolling with the punches, and of non-doing, is called *wu wei* in Chinese philosophical Taoism.

At times are are prevented from understanding the hexagrams because we fear that they will require us to undertake something beyond our capabilities, or will require something inappropriate of us. While our task may be difficult to accomplish, it is never beyond our capabilities, and never inappropriate. The Sage consistently directs us toward the good. As our experiences confirm this fact again and again, we gradually build a firm sense of trust; eventually, our distrust of the Creative is totally dismissed. A firm sense of trust is what the *I Ching* calls the power of inner truth. Being in possession of the power of inner truth, we are able to influence other people and situations toward the good. The fifth line of *Inner Truth* (61) says, "He possesses truth, which links together." This theme is discussed in *Enthusiasm* (16) which says that enthusiasm begins a movement which meets with devotion, thus carries all with it. The fourth line describes a man who "is able to awaken enthusiasm through his own sureness and freedom from hesitation.... He has no doubts and is wholly sincere," therefore, "he achieves great things."

Other obstructions to our understanding are due to untrue cultural precepts we hold. When we speak with a higher being we cannot expect to find that the values we have taken for granted as true are true from the Cosmic Viewpoint. When we hold to a culturally decadent idea, we get the hexagram *Work on What Has Been Spoiled* (18). This counsels us to search our minds to find and rid ourselves of the spoiled idea. For example, from the point of view of the *I Ching,* we aren't obligated to like people, but it is essential to disperse our dislike of them. Similarly, we may say "no" to people on grounds of intuition alone; we don't have to have reasons. Neither do we owe people trust before they have established their trustworthiness, but we do owe them an open-mind until they communicate that they are not yet meant to be trusted. They communicate their untrustworthiness to us either by outright expressions of insensitivity or moral carelessness, or by feelings of caution they arouse in us by way of intuition. Even though we receive such warnings, the *I Ching* would not have us brand them permanently as "untrustworthy people." Mentally fixing, or branding others is what the *I Ching* calls "executing people." In *The Wanderer* (56) it says that penalties and lawsuits "should be a quickly passing matter, and must not be dragged out indefinitely. Prisons ought to be places where people are lodged only temporarily, as guests are. They must not become dwelling places."

Sometimes we experience what can only be called a "rude awakening," as when we press our views on others, or strive for personal gain, or interfere in other people's business, telling them what do to. Such actions violate the Cosmic Laws, and are seen as arrogance at its worst. The rude awakenings are felt as various types of shock, or as being placed in a humiliating position. We don't know that it is a Cosmic Lesson until we consult the *I Ching* and receive a line such as the second in *Biting Through* (21), which says, "... one encounters a hardened sinner, and, aroused by anger, one goes a little too far... there is no great harm in this, because the penalty as such is just."

There are times when our hexagrams call for making a "sacrifice." When we give up feelings to which we think we are entitled, such as anger and impatience, we make a sacrifice that is for the good of the situation. Such sacrifices are called for at difficult times, as when another person is committing injustices and we are experiencing many emotions. Nevertheless, such sacrifices, selflessly offered, are true nourishment for the gods. When we sacrifice such feelings as anger, and retreat into neutrality and reserve, we often cause the offender to feel a sense of shame. Neutrality acts as a mirror in which the offending person sees his act in its true light. Moreover, because we have refrained from judgment, he is given space in which to judge himself; this enables him to retreat from evil without being blocked by shame imposed on him from without. The only way anyone is motivated to change his bad habits is by seeing his actions as they truly are. The third line in *Standstill* (12) says, "They bear shame," explaining, "inferior people who have risen to power illegitimately do not feel equal to the responsibility they have taken upon themselves. In their hearts they begin to be ashamed, although at first they do not show it outwardly. This marks a turn for the better." In keeping with the spirit of sacrifice, it is necessary to make sure our inferiors are not allowed to watch the offending person to see if he is "improving." If we do so, our ego, with its measuring, interferes. It is in keeping with another person's dignity that he does not respond to the demands of our ego. As the fourth line of *Revolution* (49) says, "Radical changes require adequate authority. A man must have inner strength as well as influential position. What he does must correspond with a higher truth and must not spring from arbitrary or petty motives; then it brings great good fortune. If a revolution is not founded on such inner truth, the results are bad, and it has no success. For in the end men will support only those undertakings which they feel instinctively to be just." Sacrificing entitlements does not mean that we "forgive and forget," but that we withdraw our dark feelings and our resistance to what is happening, and remain aware that such behavior may recur until the person has the insight and volition to correct his fault. Through withdrawing into empty space, we preserve our dignity and purity, and give the other person's superior nature support for rescuing himself.

On consulting the Sage regularly, we become aware we are communicating with one who is consistent in his way of relating to us. We see that he relates so as to constantly preserve his dignity and correctness. If we ask questions and then dismiss his advice, he will soon communicate that we, in being insensitive, cause harm, and that he can only give himself fully and freely when we are open and sensitive.

Even though we are aware of his distinct personality, the Sage resists identification. Any wish on our part to assign images to him comes from our ego, and its desires. In its glory-seeking, the ego wants to be God's right hand man, if not God himself. The Sage, however, will have nothing to do with the factionalism and elitism of our ego. In the images we receive in meditation, the Sage is either blank-faced, or takes on one image or another for the purpose of letting us know something specific. If we can content ourselves with leaving the identity of the Sage in the area of the unknown, we can come into harmony with the Cosmic Viewpoint. As Lao Tzu said, "Tao can be talked about, but not the Eternal Tao. Names can be named, but not the Eternal Name."

The Sage will answer our questions, but not in terms that would in any way compromise his principles. For instance, if we ask questions about "sex," he will not answer in those terms. Instead, he speaks of "fellowship with men" as a general principle, causing us to contemplate the essentials of correct relationships; then he speaks of the beard on the chin as a vanity to which we pay attention as opposed to the chin as the more essential thing. Gradually, we understand that we are not to think of "sex" as a thing in itself, but as an ornament of a more important and carefully developed relationship which has all the essentials of equality, justice, and sensitivity fully in place. Moreover, in our conduct, we are to reserve giving ourselves until the basis of equality and justice is firmly established. Our firmness in adhering to this standard of conduct is to "draw out the allotted time," described in the fourth line of *The Marrying Maiden* (54). To give ourselves on the basis of desire when these essentials are not securely in place is to be enslaved by our own inner weakness. From the Cosmic Viewpoint, sex as a thing in itself is a vanity created by the ego-self-image, and indulgence in it is a form of narcissism unworthy of being noticed by the Sage.

The Sage is polite, but firm in stating cosmic principles. It is through such firmness that we perceive his total personality as gentle, kind, firm, and correct—one that believes in us in spite of our deviations. He waits while we exhaust our enthusiasm for false ideas; he allows us to self-destruct if we stubbornly insist upon doing so, but would rather we did not, because, as he tells us, we have the potential for achieving something both great and permanent for the good of all, if we will do it.

While working with the Sage, we feel a nourishing, helpful presence. If we become arrogant, however, this presence departs and we begin to feel lonely. We are hardly aware of this presence until we lose it and miss it. When we return to our path, the presence gradually returns. It is as if an inner light comes and goes. By his coming and his going, he teaches us about himself and about our relationship with him.

A number of lines in the *I Ching* refer to the phenomenon of this presence. We tend to get them during times of loneliness. The first line in *The Well* (48) says, "If a man wanders around in swampy lowlands, his life is submerged in mud. Such a man loses all significance for mankind. He who throws himself away is no longer sought out by others. In the end no one troubles about him any

71

more." The sixth line in *The Wanderer* (56) says, "The bird's nest burns up," referring to our having lost the Sage's helpful protection because we insist on leading rather than following. Similar lines refer to our return to the path and the consequent return of the presence. The fourth line in *Return* (24) says, "A man is in a society composed of inferior people, but is connected spiritually with a strong and good friend, and this makes him turn back alone. Although nothing is said of reward and punishment, this return is certainly favorable, for such a resolve to choose the good brings its own reward." Another such line is the fifth line of *Grace* (22): "A man withdraws from contact with people of the lowlands, who seek nothing but magnificence and luxury, into the solitude of the heights. There he finds an individual to look up to, whom he would like to have as a friend. But the gifts he has to offer are poor and few, so that he feels ashamed. However, it is not the material gifts that count, but sincerity of feeling, and so all goes well in the end."

By developing ourselves, the *I Ching* says we are also building a home and position of importance in the inner world. *The Wanderer* (56) concerns our lonely inner world existence in which we are without friends and connections, but if we relate properly we "find friends who recommend us," and we enter the "service of a prince" who "accepts us" and "confers an office" upon us. But whenever we leave the path, "the wanderer's inn burns down." We are never quite secure in this strange land.

Still another aspect of our relationship with the Sage is our tendency to depart from the path, then return to it. We go to the Sage because we need help, but after being helped, we begin to feel we no longer need the Sage, and forget our self-development. Or, we leave the path because each new lesson is difficult. There is always the feeling of risk, as in learning to fly an airplane. One is glad to have the plane safely back on the ground and tied down. We aren't sure we want the next lesson, because each new lesson exposes us to dangers for which we must develop adequate, cool-headed responses. Thus we learn how to stall a plane and start the engine in mid-air. We learn how to slip sideways and how to spin, and how to come out of a spin. We simulate all sorts of dangerous situations in order to know how to deal with them safely.

72

These maneuvers disturb our center of gravity and we may get air-sick from the tensions and danger. It is the same with learning from life, which is to learn from the Sage. We often want to pause in our progress, or even quit and relax and enjoy things. We look forward to the time when we won't have to take any more risks—tie the life experience down and not fly anymore. When we stay in the same place, spiritually, we stagnate. Indolence takes over; we deviate from our path and become self-indulgent; we lose our seriousness of purpose and take up other people's space. The Sage, meanwhile, realizes that we will deviate. He knows how to wait. If we totally lose the way, it is entirely up to us to return. When we do return, we find that the Sage is pleased. In following his path, the Sage has withdrawn from evil in us, yet never given up on us. By preserving his integrity, he has drawn us to return. We may find ourselves gently chided by the following line in *Return* (24): "There are people of a certain inner instability who feel a constant urge to reverse themselves. There is danger in continually deserting the good because of uncontrolled desires, then turning back to it again because of a better resolution. However, since this does not lead to habituation in evil, a general inclination to overcome the defect is not wholly excluded." We begin to realize, by leaving the path and returning to it, the reliability, the absolute steadiness and unfailing compassion of the Sage.

Through coming to know the Sage, we find that the Sage plays no favorites. We are never allowed to skip steps in our development, nor are we exempted from learning any lessons (because they are hard) or from correcting any mistakes. This Sage is unlike our human teachers who sometimes give us advantages we don't deserve because they fall prey to our charm or our devices. No bargains are made with us to get us to rescue ourselves or others, or to try to do a good job. We are not even pitied when we feel self-pity. If we feel grief we are counseled, "give preponderance to grief," and we will be helped, but we will not be coddled. Perhaps this is what Lao Tzu meant when he said, "The Sage treats all men as straw dogs."

In time we come to abandon the path less often in any substantial way. Then our problems seem to result from smaller faults which diminish our inner power. The way of the Sage gradually becomes "our way," and we learn to rely on the power of our personality, and to preserve and refresh this power in each different situation.

The relationship between the Sage and ourselves is that of master and pupil, guru and follower. The guru acts as a mirror and example; through watching the guru, the follower begins to see himself. The Sage, likewise, by believing in us and presenting problems to us, and by allowing us to come and go, acts as a mirror in which we may see ourselves. By this I do not mean a mirror of vanity, in which we may admire and approve of ourselves. This mirror is more opaque than shiny, and may not be looked into directly. It catches our peripheral view, where our inferior man is caught in his dark place within. All this the Sage does without doing, by remaining empty and blank.

The Sage does not want us to be servile; he does not tell us what to think so that we merely imitate goodness; he gives hints. We must find out in our hearts what is truly good, by our efforts. Although there is a difference between himself and us, he does not want us to kneel before him and worship him, but to preserve and guard our dignity as sacred—the light and bright gift of God within. In a mediation experience I saw myself kneeling before the Sage in the belief that this must be proper. But the Sage gently took my hands and had me rise, instructing me never to lose my inner dignity, not even before him.

Another, earlier meditation answered my incessant wish to know who the Sage was. I saw a somewhat plump mandarin with a cap and pigtails sitting in a yoga position. There was something unpleasant about this image; everything but the eyes seemed a bit plastic, however, the eyes were sharp and bright. It worried me to think that this might be the Sage. Then the image changed to a long-faced western, middle-aged man I can only describe as "blubbery." Again, the face appeared to be plastic and the eyes were sharp and bright. As I began to worry that this image might be the Sage, the image changed again, this time to the figure of Christ standing, with one arm outstretched, beside a river—a picture I had seen many times in Sunday School as a child. Even though the eyes were the same, and the figure strangely plastic, as before, I hastened to kneel and worship him, grasping him about the knees. Alas, the whole image was nothing but air, which was extremely disappointing. This image was then replaced by a strong light which filled my entire field of vision, then gradually receded until it became one of the bright stars in a whole field of stars. As I pondered these images, I realized that all of the faces were masks behind which the same sharp, intense, bright eyes of the Sage could be seen. The first two images represented my fear that the Sage might be someone totally foreign to me, from whom I would ever feel isolated; the third figure—that of Christ—was what I wanted him to be. All were incorrect, as the verbal explanation that followed these images explained. I wanted some image of the Sage because I thought I needed an image, but if I must have an image, the most correct one would be that of the bright light, which represented a person who has perfected his nature; he is one of possibly millions of people who have also perfected their natures. These are what the *I Ching* calls the "ancestors"—those who have gone before us in completing their inner journey of self-development. The realization that so many people have overcome their fears and persevered through challenges and difficulties to realize their complete natures was extremely enlightening to me. Up until then, I thought that only a Christ or a Buddha, or a Lao Tzu had perfected himself. Then I realized that a mechanic I had known down the street, who set an example of correctness and humility throughout his life, was undoubtedly one in that field of stars. It was also clear that the Sage belongs to no factions, even though the Sage may permit himself to appear, as the eyes did, behind the mask of a Christ or a Buddha, to help sincere people who, as yet, have no other way to perceive him.

When I thought about it, I realized that my demand that the Sage have an identify was childish and inferior. Was it not enough to realize that the Sage is unfailingly good and unfailingly caring?

5.

Self-Development

The *I Ching* may be used in two different ways—in an occasional manner to solve momentary crises and put problems in perspective, or in a daily manner for the purpose of self-development. In the latter case, the *I Ching* becomes a manual for developing the superior man within, fitting us to become a servant of the higher power in the creative work of the world.

The *I Ching* makes it clear, in a variety of lines, that it is not enough to want to serve; we must submit ourselves to the training or self-development required. The second line of *Oppression* (47) says, "One is oppressed while at meat and drink. The man with the scarlet knee bands is just coming. It furthers one to offer sacrifice. To set forth brings misfortune. No blame." The commentary explains that before one can be of service to the prince (the one with the scarlet knee bands) "obstructions must be overcome," which must be met "in the invisible realm by offerings and prayer. To set forth without being prepared would be disastrous, though not morally wrong." Even though we may think we are very well prepared to serve the higher power, this may not be the point of view of the Sage. The fact is that during the course of our training we are given spiritual work that enables us to be of use to other people, but the work comes to us—we do not go to it—and it increases in variety and scope as we are more capable of handling it.

The fourth line in *The Well* (48) comments on the training period we must go through: "In life there are times when a man must put himself in order. During such a time he can do nothing for others, but his work is nonetheless valuable, because by enhancing his powers and abilities through inner development, he can accomplish all the more later on."

The *I Ching* makes it clear, in *Gathering Together* (45) that the ultimate goal is the unity of mankind, and that "only

76

collective moral force can unite the world." Human leaders are necessary to serve as the centers of each group. Each leader "must first of all be collected within himself." Such a leader must have strength and constancy of character, and "work unselfishly to bring about general unity." Because he sees with clarity what needs to be done, he is chosen (by the Sage) for a position of leadership, but he is capable of accomplishing his work only if he has developed the necessary attributes of character. As the fourth line of *The Ting* (50) puts it, when we fail to go about this work properly, "The legs of the *ting* are broken. The prince's meal is spilled and his person is soiled. Misfortune." The commentary explains, "A man has a difficult and responsible task to which he is not adequate. Moreover, he does not devote himself to it with all his strength but goes about with inferior people; therefore the execution of the work fails. In this way he also incurs personal opprobrium. Confucius says about this line: 'Weak character coupled with honored place, meager knowledge with large plans, limited powers with heavy responsibility, will seldom escape disaster'."

To develop the needed attributes the hexagram *Following* (17) explains that "if a man would rule he must first learn to serve, for only in this way does he secure from those below him the joyous assent that is necessary if they are to follow him." The work of self-development is that of learning to serve the higher power and be led by it. We start at the bottom in the most menial position; gradually, by freeing ourselves from faulty habits that are dangerous in positions of leadership, we are given positions of importance and influence. When our character is fully developed, every thought, every word, and every deed has power. Our influence is automatic, without requiring the slightest intention, and what we accomplish by putting ourselves in the direct line of the Creative thrust, is the Creative work in the world toward unity and harmony between people and all things.

The *I Ching* once answered my query as to what constitutes the fully developed person with the hexagram *Shock* (51), which depicts a man who, although the shock reverberates a hundred miles around, remains so composed that he does not "let fall the sacrificial spoon and chalice." Indeed, this is the image of perfect alignment with the Cosmic Will, or

Tao. It is a harmony with the shocking events happening, and a complete acceptance, without being the least perturbed or unsettled by doubt. It is only possible to come to such an acceptance by acquiring, through experience at the deepest level of awareness, an understanding of the hidden forces at work in our lives.

The second line of *Approach* (19) speaks of the inner certainty and composure of the developed person: "When a man has the inner strength and consistency that need no admonition, good fortune will ensue. Nor need the future cause any concern. He is well aware that everything earthly is transitory, and that a descent follows upon every rise, but need not be confused by this universal law of fate. Everything serves to further. Therefore he will travel the paths of life swiftly, honestly, and valiently." It is a constancy of character, capable of enduring through every challenge, that we need if we are to serve that which is higher than ourselves. Only when we are utterly reliable can we complete the work given us in a manner satisfactory both to ourselves and the Sage.

If we choose the path of self-development, we are made aware that the ordinary rules of life no longer apply to us. Conventional ways of influencing others by calling attention to our abilities and seeking prominent positions, of offering what we know and defending ourselves, must be abandoned, along with our customary reactions to the inferior behavior and mistakes of others. Where we previously defended ourselves with arguments, or by using our legal rights to force others to perform their agreements with us, we are now restricted to the means of the Sage—that of influencing and defending ourselves through modesty and inner power. From the viewpoint of our inferiors and ego, we are defenseless. Every time we abandon our new way and return to the conventional defenses, we lose the path and suffer conflict and remorse. Our new path is that of the "wanderer" who (as described in *The Wanderer* (56)) makes his way through the world as a stranger. "When a man is a wanderer and stranger, he should not be gruff nor overbearing. He has no large circle of acquaintances, therefore he should not give himself airs. He must be cautious and reserved; in this way he protects himself from evil. If he is obliging towards others, he wins success."

The superior man does not rely on logically derived thought, nor does he seek to be recognized for his wit, sharpness, or cleverness. He does not prove his superiority in debate, or engage in verbal conflict; he does not put his intellect or his learning forward, or strive to impress others with his accomplishments. All such conscious effort is considered brilliance in the *I Ching,* and the path of brilliance and show is the high road as opposed to the low road of spontaneity that arises from sincerity and humility. Like the Sage, the superior man is content to stay in the background and only be forced forward by events; he relies on what comes to him to say or do from the inner source. This simplicity and humility is called "true grace."

To be in harmony with the Cosmic Will, or Tao, is to acquiesce in whatever presents itself, as if one were the actor in a play. The action of the play carries the plot toward a final, meaningful conclusion. Here, the playwright is the Sage, or the Creative Power. As a participant in the drama, it is important to be called into action only when the moment directly involves us; our actions should be to the essence of the matter in which we find ourselves, taking on no more or less a part than the situation requires. This means we remain flexible and content, sometimes understood, sometimes misunderstood, but always aiming to respond in a way that serves the good and the true. By being used as the playwright sees fit, we enable him to bring the meaning of the play into focus, for he alone knows how to harmonize the diverse elements. The action of the play is the great Tao, an ever-moving, dynamic stream. Our job is to flow with it, align ourselves with it and allow ourselves to be used by it. Only the highly developed person can have such an attitude. The work of the *I Ching* is to develop this attitude, and to help us realize that the Sage knows how to make the play work out. As in Shakespeare's *All's Well That Ends Well,* the plot unravels and the threats subside; all the misdemeanors and shortcomings are forgiven and swept away. The superior man attains the superior place and the inferior man is put down after usurping the superior man's place. All's well and it ends well. That is the way of the Sage, as the developing person comes to know him, and the way of Tao. When we are capable of knowing the Tao from within, we can stand firmly and securely in the midst of danger.

During our training we are faced with situations which call forth our hidden doubts from their hiding places. Each confrontation, although difficult, occurs in such a manner that we are able to defeat the doubts. The fourth line of *Development* (53) compares the student to the wild goose when it has no other place to rest than on the branch of a tree—an unsuitable place for a goose. "If it is clever, it will find a flat branch on which it can get a footing. A man's life, too, in the course of its development, often brings him into inappropriate situations, in which he finds it difficult to hold his own without danger. Then it is important to be sensible and yielding. This enables him to discover a safe place in which life can go on, although he may be surrounded by danger." In following this counsel, the student learns to respond in the way of the defenseless wanderer, and he finds the help he needs to deal with the situation. This help comes from the higher source, and is available because he jeopardizes himself to rely on whatever happens. Very often the solution comes only at the very last minute, or what the ego would say was "a day late."

Self-development is also like peeling off extra layers of clothing. The extraneous matter are those pacts we make to respond to things in a certain way, and our learned responses. At first we may feel a little exposed, but with the increased activity, we soon feel warmer. For example, we have been taught to plan, to anticipate problems and to prepare responses; we even prepare our opinions before we enter situations in order to be firm in our attitudes. In the game of tennis, advanced players are trained to develop the responses that have the greatest chance of winning. Under certain conditions it is considered more desirable to serve down the line, or to return the ball cross-court. Because players tend to become "grooved" in making these plays, it is simple for those who understand these techniques, yet stay open in their own approach, to beat them. This is one of the problems in pre-structuring our responses to situations.

The student of the Sage learns to refuse the programs offered by our habitually planning mind (inferiors) and to keep his mind open and unstructured. An attitude that fastens on the needs of the moment, and upon the problems upon which we can actually have some impact, is the most creative attitude. It is freed of the doubt implied in 'looking ahead', in which our plans are but barricades against what "might happen." Indeed, either to 'look ahead', or to enviously compare ourselves with others by 'looking aside', or to measure our progress by 'looking behind', is regarded as nourishing ourselves on inferior food in the hexagram *Nourishment* (27) The images we mentally entertain by such "looking" have the bad effect of pulling us off our inner center, making us unstable and causing us to lose our path. A correct attitude is such as that required of the pilot of an airplane. Even if his airplane is new and has been repeatedly tested for failure, he does his own pre-flight check. During his flight he maintains a cautious and watchful mind, free of presumption. He knows the dangers that unexpected conditions can bring, and so is ready for what may come; he is neither anxious nor fearful.

The fourth line of *Inner Truth* (61) compares 'looking aside' to the "team horse" that "goes astray." By turning our attention aside to watch our teammate's progress, we do not walk our own path well. Moreover, we subject them to our doubt that they can manage by themselves. If we are impatient because others are not progressing at a rate that our inferiors can measure, we doubt their ability and that of the Creative to "work things out." Inner watching causes us to "want" things to be better, and all "wanting" disturbs our inner equilibrium. If we were to see ourselves "wanting" in meditation, we would see that we lean toward our wants and desires like the Leaning Tower of Pisa, instead of being centered and at rest within! The source of inner power lies in being serene and secure in one's person.

'Looking aside' is always an activity of our inferiors. Our superior self only looks at what is immediately before it. When we watch another person's behavior four things may be observed: If the person seems to be escaping bad effects from doing something wrong, our inferiors enviously observe that "we" aren't allowed to get away with being incorrect; a complaint or doubt enters our mind that Fate, or life, is unfair—that things do not "work out," at least to our satisfaction. This misunderstanding causes us to feel isolated and to think of leaving the path of patient perseverance—to "do something" about the apparent injustice; we think of taking matters into our own hands to condemn that person, or to disbelieve in the justice and power of the Creative. Such a doubt must then be dealt with. Second, our inferiors measure another person's progress with the idea that they will be disciplined and allow themselves to be led only on the condition that doing so will lead to an observable change in the other person's behavior. When that rate of progress is not measurable, our inferiors rebel and threaten to leave the path. Third, because our inferiors demand that the other person conform to their expectations, the other person may not respond, because it is in keeping with his spiritual dignity not to respond to the demands of anyone's inferiors. In this case the presence of our inferiors keeps what we want to happen from happening. Fourth, the threat on the part of our inferiors that they will leave the path is aimed at the Sage, which causes us to lose our partnership with him, for the Sage must retreat when our inferiors seize leadership in this manner. All of these problems are best corrected at the very beginning, when we are first tempted to 'look aside' to see what other people are doing. Finally another person may, for reasons put forward by his own inferiors, try to get us to 'look aside' at what he is doing. It is important to stay unengaged, keeping the complaints of our inferiors under control. The *I Ching,* in the hexagram *Dispersion* (59), speaks of dispersing feelings of alienation and anger, or sacrificing these feelings to the higher power, for the good of the situation. Such images are very helpful in dealing with situations of this kind.

On recognizing that we have turned our affairs over to our inferiors, we then need to be tolerant of ourselves. The *I Ching* makes it clear in *Youthful Folly* (4) that we cannot expect to know everything about the inner world in advance. It is immodest to expect too much at once, as *Duration* (32) says, advising us not to be put off by our failures. To "wrestle" with a fate that has been years in the making is the challenge of a blind and lame man, as *Treading* (10) reminds

82

us. We need only keep steadily on the path, without measuring ourselves against some preconceived image of ability or inability. Our ego does such measuring, and would discourage us from undertaking a development that would end its leadership.

When we see that because of our mistakes we have slipped backwards, losing the ground we so carefully gained, our inferiors become alarmed, and pride is aroused. After all, they think they have truly been humble, have truly been conscientious, and now all they worked for has evaporated like water. The *I Ching* counsels us to "be modest about our modesty," to forgo pride and return to the path. It is the only correct thing to do, and everyone who has ever been on the path has had to return, without any reason whatsoever.

Obviously, self-development frequently requires us to endure stressful situations. This seems to be the only means by which what we know through the intellect can be transformed into "knowledge of the heart," or "inner truth." Only by arousing our fears can we bring them to the surface to deal with them; only by being tested do we develop the constancy of character needed to be of use; only by being emotionally jeopardized are we able to subjugate our inferiors. The fact that we seem to be able to learn only in this manner must have provoked Lao Tzu to speak of "prizing adversity," humorously mentioning the later surprise of being free of it. The *I Ching*, in *The Taming Power of the Great* (26) compares our going through such trying situations to practicing "chariot driving."

Contrary to what we might believe, there is a negative aspect in stopping to count our blessings; in doing so we 'look behind' at progress gained, and 'look aside' at our current situation, and in the process we engage our ego and its preferences. There is an element of congratulation in being thankful that we are not among the hungry, poor, or handicapped. The Sage would have us accept the condition we are in with equanimity, and make the best of it. It is important, on having good luck, to keep joy in bounds, as one line in the *I Ching* puts it. We take care not to be proud that we are well-off, or indulge feelings of self-pity if we are poor. In counting our blessings we single out preferences and then become factional about them. We may have a "favorite dog," or tree, or flower, or child, or group of people. We may think of ourselves inflexibly as being either a "city person" or a "country person," or one who "cannot live alone," or one who "cannot live with anyone." All these images are caused by attachments which prevent us from accepting life as it comes, with equanimity; in adhering to these attachments we indulge a certain vanity, prizing the way we feel. In prizing the way we feel, we may regard our good feelings about others as a magnificent gift we bestow upon them; then their good regard for us is obscured and we no longer look at them as equals. It is in such subtle ways that we lose our humility and acceptance of life. In correcting our character we accept rain as well as sunshine, winter as well as summer, and activity as well as rest. We free ourselves from our petty likes and dislikes—those impurities of character that obscure the true greatness which we are. Our inferiors may read these lines in their extreme and wonder whether we must like mosquitos and ticks as well as our pets! However, we need to find the common-sense in all these ideas that expresses itself in a moderate, just, and detached point of view. Strangely enough, on attaining a detached view, the things we most enjoy begin to happen to us, until once more we "count our blessings" and attach ourselves to having them. This is the way of Fate.

'Looking behind' has all the faults of 'looking ahead', 'looking aside', and 'looking at' our situation. Through being open and unstructured, we draw the help of the Creative to overcome difficulties, but then in 'looking behind', we reconsider, thinking that we (our ego) really made the progress by virtue of our intelligence. If we fall victim to this vanity we find that our progress deteriorates and we are confronted with more difficulties. We are warned in *After Completion* (63) that once the pressure caused by adversity begins to let up, the ego returns in the form of renewed self-confidence. It replays the situation before our mind's eye, replacing the Creative with itself as the hero of the hour. If this is too absurd, the ego puts forth the argument that we overestimated the situation—"it would have got better on its own." The ego denigrates everything in our attitude that was modest and conscientious—all the elements by which we attained the help of the Creative. The sixth line of *After Com-*

pletion warns us against such self-confidence: "After crossing a stream, a man's head can get into the water only if he is so imprudent as to turn back.... There is a fascination in standing still and looking back over a peril overcome. However, such vain self-admiration brings misfortune. It leads only to danger, and unless one finally resolves to go forward without pausing, one falls a victim to this danger." The correct attitude is described in the sixth line of *Possession In Great Measure* (14): "In the fullness of possession and at the height of power, one remains modest and gives honor to the Sage who stands outside the affairs of the world. By this means one puts oneself under the beneficent influence descending from heaven, and all goes well."

Other aspects of 'looking behind' are discussed in the third and fifth lines of *After Completion*. The third line gives the analogy of the Emperor Wu Ting's having "waged long colonial wars for the subjection of the Huns who occupied the northern borderland with constant threat of incursions." The commentary stresses that "a correct colonial policy is especially important. The territory won at such bitter cost must not be regarded as an almshouse for people who in one way or another have made themselves impossible at home, but who are thought to be quite good enough for the colonies." Applied to personal affairs, if after we have corrected our relationship with another person by strictly avoiding arguments, we then allow ourselves to engage in arguing with them, we allow our inferiors to rule once more. We may not allow the subjugated inferior element either in ourselves or in other people to reassert itself.

The fifth line of *After Completion* calls attention to the tendency, once we have made a relationship correct through maintaining reserve, to then re-consider, thinking, "I've been too hard on them," by which we return to an easy-going, casual attitude. Not only have our inferiors been waiting on the side to enjoy the situation, whether it is correct or not, but this attitude is what the *I Ching* calls "magnificent." We play God by granting heavenly favors and pardons when we don't have the right to do so. A similar arrogance occurs when we let someone (of reasonable ability) win at tennis because we play better than they do. Our duty is to require others to do their best, or allow them to do what they will, but not assume

85

that they can't win on their own, or that they won't improve if we don't coddle them.

Even if we don't adopt grandiose attitudes through 'looking behind', we tend to forget our responsibility to maintain the correct reserve with someone when they begin to relate correctly to us. The third line in *Grace* (22) warns us not to "sink into convivial indolence, but to remain constant in perseverance. Good fortune depends on this." Similarly, the fifth line in *Biting Through* (21) (a hexagram that concerns dealing with other people's inferior behavior) says, "The case to be decided is indeed not easy but perfectly clear. Since we naturally incline to leniency, we must make every effort to be like yellow gold—that is, as true as gold and as impartial as yellow, the color of the middle [the mean]. It is only by remaining conscious of the dangers growing out of the responsibility we have assumed that we can avoid making mistakes." Bad habits in others are not changed in a day. Before we can let go of our reserve, the person must have truly and permanently corrected his attitude, from his own insight and volition.

Freeing our mind (what we focus on and listen to within) of the dominance of the ego and our inferiors is part of the work by which we re-attain our natural state of innocence. Through self-discipline, we keep our mind's eye open, and our inner space free of the thoughts that our inferiors would introduce if we fail to resist them. In the time of youth we are automatically open-minded; it is unnecessary to make a conscious effort to be so. After we learn structured ways of dealing with the world, and listen to the urgings of our fears, our inner view becomes blocked and our inner space filled. We are no longer able to see or hear within, but are attuned only to the external world and how we think we need to be to deal with it. Through self-development we de-structure our patterned ways of thinking; by conscious effort we keep our inner view and inner space empty. In this manner we reconstruct our original innocence. The only difference is that our new innocence is consciously maintained; it is not the unconscious innocence of childhood.

The effort required entails overcoming the comfortable easiness of relying on pre-set attitudes. Indolence makes such changes difficult, but they are even more so if our attitudes seem sufficient. Self-development is usually undertaken when we begin to see that we lack the answers we need to deal adequately with life. The hexagrams counsel us to sacrifice these preset attitudes and learn to rely on the Unknown. We are to remain open and unstructured even though the pressure of circumstance may be very strong, tempting us to fall back on the old defenses. *Preponderance of the Small* (62) mainly concerns our remaining in the undecided, ambiguous area at a time when the pressure is great for us to make some sort of move. *The Taming Power of the Great* (26) gives counsel for dealing with the build-up of this pressure, which is mainly to hold firm and keep still within, letting the situation build without interfering. If we persevere, accepting what happens as it happens, the intuitive response is able to break through, and we find that this response is not only sufficient to meet the situation, but has a perfect appropriateness that could not have been contrived through wit and cleverness. By following this course of action, our response is that described in the first line of *Innocence* (25): "The original impulses of the heart are always good, so that we may follow them confidently, assured of good fortune and achievement of our aims."

Only by keeping our inner eye open and the voices of our inferiors stilled are we able to receive the deeper, intuitive responses. To understand how this works we need to investigate the intuitive faculty. To know intuitively is to know something without having thought about it. We know something in the same way that our body knows whan an object is incompatible with it, as when in surgery, bone is transplanted, or metal objects are inserted into joints for support. The body knows this compatibility down to the degree of correspondence or rejection; it accepts things outright, partially, or not at all. Similarly, our intuition acts as an "early warning system," alerting us to the approach of an incompatible image or situation; it also acknowledges when other images and situations are acceptable. However, once we let an objectionable thing pass through, by rationalizing it, the intuition seems to disappear, except for occasional outbursts when we are placed in extreme danger. Even these grow inaudible if we no longer pay heed. Intuitive knowledge is absolutely free of emotion and objective in tone, even when it sounds an alarm, as in "Be still!" "Be careful!" "Do not move!'' The reactions of our inferiors vary, depending upon our level of growth. If we have rationalized such warnings away, we may continue to treat them with indifference, but if our superior nature is developed, we become alert and watchful.

The rejection or acceptance that the intuition inspires occurs on such a deep level that we often speak of the way we feel as a "gut reaction," or "I feel it in my bones," as a way of describing its harmony with our true nature. If we are able to listen to intuition, we find that we reject that which is untrue in an outright manner. To quarrel with it is to produce inner conflict and a deep sense of unease. Conversely, acceptance of what is true produces relief.

We are able to listen to intuition only by being free of our inferiors. This is why, in *The Clinging* (30) it is said that we may attain clarity only by allowing ourselves to be docile and empty within. Looking and listening to the empty space within, we are both aware of the external world (in a detached way) and open to the cosmos, where everything of benefit to our situation is available to us.

Our original nature is like a well built dory capable of going through gigantic waves; however, through fear, we have added devices to it until it has become so weighted that the first storm is likely to swamp it. Cultural precepts founded on doubt and fear are like devices on the dory; they interfere with the natural design and obstruct the smooth, natural order of change. By adding pretenses and defenses, we become fundamentally unsuited to the demands of life. These pretenses and defenses not only make us indifferent to others, they cause us to make demands, taking up other people's physical and psychological space. When entire classes of society do this, widespread suffering results, and harmony and order cannot be achieved. The only remedy is for each person who sees the need, to undertake self-development; then he acts as a center of a group, setting a beneficial example to everyone he knows by how he meets each daily circumstance. By returning to simplicity and sincerity himself, he enables others to give up their defenses and pretenses. By being reliable and enduring in his virtue, he brings out the superior man in others and helps them give up their fears.

Through self-development our attitudes and our will are

slowly reattuned to the Cosmic Will. Those attitudes that have been weakened by indifference and indolence are revitalized and restored; we return to our original state of careful conscientiousness and sincerity. Developing our superior nature is like tuning a piano to concert pitch after it has sagged. The entire dynamics of the piano are lifted and harmonized. At first this puts great pressure on the strings and harp, therefore the work must be done slowly and carefully, allowing the new condition to settle.

Through opening ourselves up to the risks of the Unknown, we begin to see how we are aided and defended by the higher power. Our spontaneous responses prove surprisingly adequate to meet each situation. In watching and listening for the entrance of our ego, with its dark-seeing and its resistance to our efforts, we acquire a certain amount of inner seeing and hearing that we forgot was possible. Through dispersing negative attitudes in response to the hexagrams, we learn the beginnings of *wu wei*—flowing with life, not resisting what happens. We may not have gone so far as to "prize calamity" but we begin to find and stay within the empty space. Through developing a careful conscientiousness we learn the meaning of modesty—not seeking to be full, to feel glad or satisfied. We learn to dwell in the low places not sought by others for we realize that nature acts to fill up what is low and to tear down what is high. We begin to realize the great power of modesty, sincerity and constancy. Through withdrawing from the ego-assaults of others, we learn to preserve our personalities and how not to engage in evil. When we do engage in conflicts we notice a loss of inner strength that we find regrettable so that we grow less satisfied with straying from the path. Little by little we put the raw material of our native potentials into a working personality, firm and strong in itself, and attuned to the Higher Will.

All the same, from time to time during our development, we allow our ego to ask, "Is the ego all that bad?" As long as this question remains unresolved, we will find ourselves constantly undermined in our progress. If we follow the path of the ego to its inevitable conclusion, we find that it is on a course in direct conflict with the life principle. Its trajectory ends in the death of the spirit. We need to understand this in all its implications in order to help ourselves and others in times of trouble, when the inner light is severely darkened.

From the Bottom of the Pit Up

For many of us there comes a time in life when the trap door of our certainties falls from under us. Up to this moment everything seems to have been successful enough, but suddenly we feel differently, and the ways in which we have been relating to situations suddenly cease to work. Contemplating the causes, we find it difficult to assign reasons. Strangely, just before this moment we have attained a high point of self-assurance, yet now our will to go on has fallen to its lowest point.

What we can scarcely realize is that the crisis has been precipitated by the sudden realization, on the part of our ego, that life is not going to work out, in the long run, in its favor. What it has based its hopes on and was willing to work toward, is really unattainable. Seeing no further reason to go on, the ego prefers a suicide of the spirit.

The *I Ching* calls this a state of exhaustion. The hexagram *Oppression (Exhaustion)* (47) compares our state to a lake that has dried up. It is a dangerous state because the power of the ego is at its strongest point, and its dominance over our will can cause us to commit the suicide that it constantly advocates in the implied threat, "If I can't have things my way, 'we' won't go on."

This state may have resulted from a general exhaustion of hopes, or an external shock such as a death, or divorce, or sudden decrease of self-image as may occur in being fired from a job, or dismembered in an accident. Any of these situations may deprive our ego of the conditions it sees as essential for living further. Exhaustion of our will to live may cause illness—a giving up that ends in cancer or other disease. If we allow these feelings to go unresisted, as if we are powerless to stop them, we may allow the death of the spirit to happen.

It is important to realize that our general feelings, both of helplessness and hopelessness, are delusions foisted upon us by our ego. As leader of our personality it gives us the impression that we are powerless against it. To make matters more difficult, our inferiors are very frightened and very vocal, taking up our inner space.

Were we to see where we are in terms of the 'inner world', we would discover that we are trapped at the bottom of a dark, deep, dry well, in the company of lizards. The sides of the well are too slippery to climb out. Externally we may be ill, even within sight of physical death. Our intuition may be heard to say, "Do you want to live or not? You must decide." This may be followed by the admonition, "What about those who depend on you? How will they get along?"

Before we fell into this dark inner place, our external life seemed to go on almost too smoothly. We seem to have had an endless license to err; we may have tested to see how far we could exercise our power and arrogance without incurring bad results. Now, everything we do has a penalty attached. It is as if we are in a straightjacket and have no license at all. Our first response is like that of a spoiled child which hits its head against the wall on being thwarted. First we try to endure the situation, then we resist it. The struggle against giving up becomes very intense; to live or die, to continue or quit?

We discover that to live we must resolutely refrain from entertaining even the slightest thought that death might be a way out. We also must be resolute against the temper-tantrums of our inferiors as they attack the limits in wave-like assaults. To them the situation seems to be a punishment for existing. This is when we tend to receive the *I Ching* line from *Darkening of the Light* (36), "Darkening of the light as with Prince Chi." The commentary explains that "in order to escape danger" those who cannot "leave their posts in times of danger.... need invincible perseverance of spirit and re-doubled caution in their dealings with the world." The sixth line in *Limitation* (60) explains that during such times "galling limitation"—is "the only means of saving one's soul, which otherwise would succumb to irresolution and temptation."

Troubled by ill health and despair, we look for spiritual solutions, for intuitively we know this is the realm in which the answer lies, but for a while our ego prompts us to try con-ventional methods of healing. People around us who have not yet experienced the fall of their inferior man urge us to con-sult the medical profession; being in a weakened state, we may be lured by hopes of quick solutions, but if we continue to ignore the spiritual route by which our inner light may be revived, we may not survive. This is not to say that death is avoidable, in the end, for it certainly will come, but it need not and should not result from having given up on life. Death is more properly the fulfillment of life, coming at the opportune time when it culminates life's meaning and gives focus to one's achievements. In this context it cannot be a desolate event but a joyful summation, even though on first glance and for some time afterward one may feel a deep sense of personal loss. When the circumstances of death are correct, grief passes into a golden hue of remembrance.

Meeting Fate as the inevitable end of going in a wrong direction produces a form of recognition that the *I Ching* calls "shock." Fate is like the sides of a wide canal—in going against our nature we bump into the sides because we are not lined up in the direction of the canal. Another glimpse of Fate in the form of shock comes in recognizing that for a long time we have played, or experimented with life to see where our limits are. The hexagram *Treading* (10) likens this to "treading on the tail of a tiger." Because the treading is playful, the hexagram explains, the tiger does not bite. But the moment we become entrenched in evil, the tiger bites. The bite of the tiger—getting caught in its jaws—is the pressure we feel in coming up sharply against our new set of limits. While still in the state of shock, we concentrate on what we think is the injustice of the situation, but it is necessary to stop resisting in this manner and to allow ourselves to be led. Every resistance is dangerous, throwing us back upon the rocks of despair and defeat, close to death. We are held in the tiger's teeth until we correct ourselves and recognize, without regressions, that life is a serious, meaningful business.

In coming to terms with Fate, the intellect is little or no use, for we are ignorant of the affairs of the inner world. *Youthful Folly* (4) makes it clear that we cannot know about the inner world in advance. We need guidance. *Difficulty at the Beginning* (3) says that if we hunt without the guidance of the forrester (the Sage) we only lose our way. To obtain help we must ask for it, sublimating our egos and allowing ourselves to be led.

To give an example of "getting caught in the tiger's

jaws" and of trying to get out purely by effort, a young man I know received a scholarship to Cornell and graduated with honors; afterwards he married the daughter of a famous man and was soon employed by a prestigious company in what might be regarded as an envious position for a man starting out in the business world. He was considered to be not only highly successful and intelligent, but also a charming, knowledgeable and graceful person. At this high point in his life he had an automobile accident. On being examined at the hospital, a splinter of jawbone pierced the main artery to his brain. In spite of immediate and competent surgery, he was paralyzed on one side of his body, and lost his ability to speak or walk. Not dwelling on his losses, he applied all his will to recovering his physical abilities. Within two years he had restored a large portion of his speech and some movements on his paralyzed side, but it became clear that he would never walk again. Perhaps more important to him, he would never recover what he thought he needed to be, in physical terms, to fulfill the role of husband and father to his wife and child. Like so many others who have had to undergo a drastic and final decrease in their self-image, he plunged into despair and eventually attempted suicide. Some time later, after a great deal of suffering, he resurrected his will to live. Through work, the strength of his original nature returned and he finally overcame the assaults of his ego. He was able, after intensely wrestling with himself, to accept the role that life forced upon him, even though these strugglings had also precipitated a divorce from his wife. Eventually, he returned to his job and began to devote himself to the problems of paraplegics. An enormous change had taken place in his assessment of the meaning of life.

An example of what happens when we fail to adapt to adverse circumstances is in the case of a woman whose husband had adored her during their early married life. At middle age he began to have numerous affairs with other women. She was unable to accept this blow to her identify and within two years contracted all three types of cancer and died. Such dangers occur when we attach ourselves with pride to belonging to a certain family, or graduating from a certain school, or belonging to a certain social class, or church, or state, or race, or nationality. It is equally dangerous to accept, in reverse, defeated images of ourselves as "being" an alcoholic, or drug addict, or ex-convict, or any other negative branding because we may have met the consequences of following a wrong path. In self-development all fixed views of ourselves, attachments to images, and defensive positions, must be sacrificed. Only then can we change these trajectories and win the defense and help of the higher power.

At the depth of despair the first things to correct are the harmful ideas with which we nourish ourselves. *Nourishment* (27) refers to these ideas, warning us against the notion that we may dally with any idea without coming to harm. It points out that every false idea we consider has the potential to affect us for the worse. *The Joyous* (58) warns us against being "sincere toward disintegrating influences" which draw us off our center balance. *Influence* (31) counsels us against listening to ideas that collapse our perseverance. Many other hexagrams similarly alert us to the destructive effects of seemingly harmless ideas that are "poor nourishment." Desires, such as wanting things to happen before their time, and doubts, such as ideas by which we visualize a situation as "hopeless," are examples of bad nourishment.

When we attend a movie, watch television or read a novel, we compare the ideas presented with our intuitive standards of truth. What we see as absurd we immediately discard. If we are undecided, however, we tend to put the idea on hold and fantasize about it. By entertaining it, the idea tends to become accepted through indolence—a sort of osmosis that occurs simply because we are not decisive against it. Because we have not yet experienced its dangerous aspects, we take the idea to be benign. Seeing it as benign, we tend to let down our guard, consequently its credibility and acceptability increases. *Coming to Meet* (44) describes this process: "The inferior thing seems so harmless and inviting that a man delights in it; it looks so small and weak that he imagines he may dally with it and come to no harm." *The Abysmal* (29) says, "By growing used to what is dangerous, a man can easily allow it to become part of him. He is familiar with it and grows used to evil. With this he has lost the right way, and misfortune is the natural result." As long as we have not actively decided against a dangerous idea, it remains potent in our idea-system. We must brand it for what it is—a lure, delusion, or half-truth capable of mischief. Because of the dangers of playing with questionable ideas, fantasy, from the *I Ching* point of view, is harmful. Decisiveness against questionable ideas is the only decision-making of significance we may do in our lives. The superior man does not brand evil in others, but in himself in order to rid himself of it.

Coping with the frustrations that come from bad nourishment is one of the subjects of *Keeping Still* (52). Only by silencing the voices of our inferiors can we remain free from the vortex of the Dark Power. Precisely when we are attacked by feelings of restlessness or helplessness we get the hexagram *Keeping Still*. By following its counsel, and that of others like it, such as *The Clinging* (30), we are able to gain detachment from our emotions and attain clarity of mind.

While the first purpose of 'keeping still' is to find inner peace through silencing our inferior voices, it is also a method of meditation unique to the *I Ching*. 'Keeping still' involves bringing the movement of the spinal nerves to a standstill. Once in this state, "the ego, with its restlessness, disappears," as the hexagram *Keeping Still* states. The fourth line of *The Receptive* (2) notes that the dark element closes when at rest. During activity, conscious thought occurs at lightening speed. However, when we cultivate inner quiet, it is as if the fast, movie-like action of our mind slows down until we are able to see the individual frames—the source images of our thought patterns. These images are stored in our computer-like memory banks. They may be true perceptions of life, untrue fantasies, or decadent traditional ideas. The truer and more relative these images are, the truer are our responses to life, because these truer images act to keep us open and unstructured in our responses. By being open and unstructured, we are able to receive the impulses that come from the inner world—those of intuition and inner truth. It is possible, through 'keeping still', to recall the primary images; if they are inadequate or untrue, we may re-decide the questions and re-program ourselves to keep open and make available an ongoing intuitive awareness. This re-programming frees us from the harmful effects of the false ideas we have stored.

It is important to state, without qualification, that we need guidance of the Sage in this inner domain of darkness. Confucius said, "To study without meditation is labor wasted; to meditate without study is perilous." My own practice has been to consult the *I Ching* in the evening and allow the hexagrams and their images to digest overnight, then meditate just after awakening. The first line of *The Clinging* (30) recommends this practice, saying, "It is precisely at the beginning that serious concentration is important, because the beginning holds the seed of all that is to follow."

In preparing to 'keep still' several steps are helpful. Gentle yoga exercises ease physical tensions which would otherwise have to be overcome by mental effort. Sitting in an erect but comfortable position keeps us awake and free of distractions. The first part of meditation should serve to bring our attention from the external world of the senses to the internal, intuitive world. This requires that we empty our inner space—the area in which our inner thoughts take place.

In *Keeping Still* it says, "The heart thinks constantly," and that it is necessary to bring the impulses of the heart to quiet. The heart, as center of our body-soul, wants things and casts about constantly. This wanting, when it cannot lead to having, makes the "heart sore," a condition especially prevalent in the depths of despair. When the heart thinks, the breath becomes short and fast. Deep yoga breathing serves to quiet the heart and still the agitation caused by incessant wanting. Four or five deep, slow, cleansing breaths seem sufficient to transfer our attention from the external to the internal world. (In yoga breathing it is considered important to exhale more slowly than we inhale.)

After breathing exercises, we may next focus on the work of "inner cleansing." This work, even if we do nothing more in meditating, is what *The Taming Power of the Great* (26) refers to as "daily self-renewal." It says that "only through such daily self-renewal can a man continue at the height of his powers." In *The Ting* (50) the first line says, "A *ting* with legs upturned. Furthers removal of stagnating stuff." The *ting* symbolizes our inner container, or inner space; what we put in this container is nourishment for God. In this cleansing work it is helpful to begin by reviewing the way we feel about other people, and see whether we resist our life as it is. If we discover negative elements, they must be sacrificed so we may attain inner quiet. It is not a temporary sacrifice but a permanent one, made for the good of the situation. In yielding these inferior things up, we enable ourselves to be led by the higher power, for the sacrifice puts us in harmony with the Sage. Since everything in our minds exists in image form, we need to form an image of a place of sacrifice—an inner altar— upon which to sacrifice our negative ideas and feelings. Doing this in image-form frees us from their pressures. Entrenched habits of mind may return and have to be sacrificed again, but each time that we give them up, they become less powerful in their ability to influence us.

If, beyond this point, we are still harassed by feelings of restlessness and resistance to meditation, our ego or inferiors are controlling things, preventing us from attaining a true state of inner quiet. The ego interrupts with "reasons to do something else that is more important." If we continue with a persevering attitude, however, its sleepy-mindedness takes over. Once we begin to be aware of our ego's efforts to distract us, we come to the point of ego-separation. Until now the ego has seemed to be us; now we hear it as if it is someone else. This awareness is our superior self looking and listening; our inner eye and inner ear are tuning in to the inner world.

The use of mental images is important both in getting to the meditation state and in meditation itself, with the difference being that we consciously use them to get into meditation, while in the meditation state what we "do" seems to happen because of suggestions we intuit. To get into the meditation state the conscious use of images are helpful. The involuntary nervous system can be influenced by the use of imagery. In voice training, for instance, it is impossible to relax the voice by thinking "relax." Therefore, voice students are sometimes taught to project their voices out to a point on the wall. This relaxes the vocal cords. Similarly, by visualizing the spinal cord and its accessory nerves as black, then shining a strong, imaginary light upon them, we may bring their activity to a standstill. This stops restless energy and the tensions caused by negative ideas. Once we have become still, so that no images or voices intrude into our inner space, we may begin to see images as if we were watching a movie. Then, anything we may "do" happens because of suggestions we hear. For example, one of my early meditations was of being in a small, dark, log cabin which had neither floor nor windows, only a doorway with no door. The dirt floor was littered with trash, and cobwebs indicated that no one had been in this cabin in ages. I noticed that a broom leaned against the wall and it came to me to sweep out the cabin, which I also realized was my "inner space." In following this suggestion I realized that I was "being led," and that if I consciously intervened, the meditation would have ended.

When we first meditate, it may take as much as an entire week of meditating to quiet restlessness. Similarly, if we stop meditating for more than a few days, extra days of meditating are required to once more achieve a true state of inner quiet. Once we have tamed restless energy, it is best to keep it controlled by daily self-renewal. The problem is no different than that of the pianist or the tight-rope walker who must practice every day.

Once we have dispersed the ego and tamed restless energy, we come to the state of inner quiet—the empty place, free of all thought. It is important to accept it for what it is—empty, with nothing in it. We expect nothing, and accept everything as it is. If we are humble, accessible and open-minded, we may experience another, unique realm of meditation.

When I first began meditating, as my hexagrams counseled me to do, I had an experience about meditating. Having come to this empty place, I then saw myself in a rather barren room with uncomfortable chairs and a sign on the wall that made me realize I was in "the doctor's office," waiting for the doctor. I sat and waited for a very long time. At length, the thought came to me, upon wondering how long I would have to wait, that perhaps waiting patiently was all I was meant to do; immediately I resolved to accept the situation as it was presented, and that while I did not get to see the doctor, just being there sufficed. Upon resigning myself to this attitude of acceptance, the doctor came in, and the meditation ended. The message was simply that an attitude of acceptance was required to obtain "the doctor's help." It was important that I feel and know from within the sense of humility that was required.

In this state of inner quiet we are able to see and hear thoughts which come from the inner world. When we meditate in conjunction with consulting the hexagrams, our meditations become learning situations like the one described.

To see in the inner world, our inner eye must be opened.

If we earnestly seek to know, this happens when we allow ourselves to be guided. As long as we have fears or hesitations, we hold back and lead, rather than allow ourselves to be led. My first experience of inner seeing occurred one morning after awakening, I had not yet arisen or attempted to meditate. Although my eyes were closed, I saw an intense light that completely filled my field of vision, then filled my body as well, as if it were only an empty shell. At first I was afraid, wondering for an instant what the light could be, for I had the sensation that the light was some sort of being. Then a voice said, "Allow this to happen, there is no harm." It was such an authoritative, calming voice that I knew it to be totally good, therefore my resistance to it gave way. Immediately I began to experience a peaceful feeling that lasted throughout that day and for some time afterwards. From that time on I was able to see in the inner world during meditation, although I did not see things every time I meditated—only when I needed to learn something, or to see with clarity.

A year later, my husband began to meditate. One day we meditated at the same time after awakening. He, as yet, had no visual or audible experiences, and I had never shared my experience of seeing that light with anyone. In my meditation that morning I saw a group of doctors, who appeared on first glance, to be operating on a man in a field. The operation had just ended and they were taking bandages off his eyes. I recognized my husband as he opened his eyes. Clearly, he could see nothing but light as he sat there and blinked. This was the end of my meditation. Soon, my husband also finished meditating and began describing the "amazing" thing that had happened to him—the intense light entering his eyes and going into his body, and the feeling of peace. From that time on he could also see in the inner world during meditation. It was in this way that I became aware that one must have one's inner eye opened.

For a long time, our work in meditation is to find hidden evils and battle with our fears. All this takes place in a "dark realm." However, one day we get past this dark realm into a sphere of light and beauty, which I can only call "the other side of life." Just as there is a dark side of the earth and a light side, depending on which side the sun shines, there also appears to be another side of life which we leave at birth and re-enter at death, and which we may visit occasionally through meditation.

Even though our meditations, for the most part, will be nothing more than the work of inner cleansing, with occasional visions and experiences, this simple daily work must not be made to appear unimportant by contrast to the luxury of the visual experiences. Renewal through meditation should be undertaken in the same way we clean our houses, or order our work benches, or our desks. Everyday life necessarily engages the dark force. Life is activity, and in our business we momentarily disorder our inner life, as our houses become disordered through using them. When living in a house makes it dirty, we must clean it and put it in order. In renewing our personalities we bring ourselves back to a state of rest and clean our inner space. Meditation restores our vital energies. Only when we are in a state of rest can we feel a sense of unity with the universe.

When we do have meditation experiences, the situations we encounter are drawn from ordinary consciousness. Other people in older cultures saw mythological beasts, but my meditations included images of submarines and computers as well as *I Ching* images such as dragons, wells, and *tings.* Dreams of a forceful or vivid nature contain meanings which may be realized by meditating afterwards.

Experiences in meditation, like dreams, are easily forgotten, so it is important to write them down, for if we meditate over a period of years we find that the experiences comprise an entire inner life journey that becomes as important as any outer world experience. For example, over the years my simple dark hut evolved into a clean Swiss chalet with a wooden floor; later it became a Victorian house which had beautiful paneling, but was rather dark. My present house is one that has much light and beds of roses blooming just outside.

Meditation experiences make us aware of the symbolism of myths and fairy tales. Snow White symbolizes our superior self organizing and disciplining the inferiors, represented by the dwarfs. The evil queen is our inferior man, or ego, with its preoccupation with how it looks. The Wicked Witch of the West in *The Wizard of Oz,* similarly, is the evil aspect of the ego, while the wizard is its unmasked bravado. Alice's shrinking to enter Wonderland symbolizes the decrease of ego which enables us to enter the inner world. The three-headed dog Cerberus, of Greek myth, is our ego on guard against our entering the underworld. Orfeus, told not to look back at Euridice as he led her out of the underworld, is hearing the same admonition we receive in *After Completion* (63)—not to "look back" over dangers overcome.

Through 'keeping still' we are able to perceive the negative images we harbor, and through conquering evil in ourselves we are able to be compassionate and forbearing with others who are caught in the same vortex of fear. We understand that it is only through being given help that we have been able to become free, therefore, we are willing to help others by being open-minded toward them, and by holding to their great potential. We are also more able to avoid the vindictiveness and intolerance that made us a part of the evil process. This is to express at some point in our lives that sublime quality of the well-developed person described in the sixth line of *The Well* (58), of the "really great man whose inner wealth is inexhaustible; the more that people draw from him, the greater his wealth becomes."

6.

Action in Human Relationships

We find that while we are working on our self-development through the *I Ching,* we are gradually realigning our point of view to the 'way of the Sage'. This point of view is in harmony with our true nature, therefore free of any internal conflict. In having the courage to sacrifice our traditional means of self-defense, we find ourselves being defended; in foregoing our traditional means of striving, by wit and by effort, to make progress against our problems, we are given a far more powerful weapon against evil when the Creative Force is activated in our behalf. What is it that defends us and serves as our weapon? Modesty. Modesty is both our shield and our sword. Modesty alone arouses the Creative Power. Through modesty, that is, through doing nothing at all, we achieve everything.

Modesty, in the *I Ching* has several meanings. First it is the humility of knowing we need help from the Sage, and asking for it. Second, it is will-power as reticence, restraining our clamoring inferiors. Third, it is patience, holding firm when the pressures of the moment are intense, and when yielding to them in the slightest degree would cause us to lose our path. Fourth, it is conscientiousness, reflecting to see if we have overlooked any evil in ourselves, and keeping on guard against the entrance of any doubt. This conscientiousness amounts to an unflagging awareness so that one is not deceived by self-flattery or false enthusiasm brought on by the pressure to find "solutions." Fifth, modesty is enduring firmly through sheer will-power as perseverance. Sixth, it is the will to accept things as they come, ever seeking clarity through acceptance and docility, for one realizes that clarity gives one the strength to see things through to completion. Finally, modesty is expressed as devotion to the path of the good for its own sake, for one sees clearly that staying on the path is the goal, and that everything good comes out of that.

Through following our path, suffering in the world is lessened, and the world is one step further towards peace and order.

At first we are unable to see any of these things with clarity, and for a time our ego believes that to drop our defenses may cast us into doom. But gradually, with growth, the power of this fear dwindles and we are able, after taking all the preliminary steps, to take our feet off the bottom and swim. We are not able to do this before the proper time comes, or without first securing the support of the Sage. For a long time we must be content to wait and work without expectation. Then this support comes. We need to realize that it can come only when we prove reliable—devoted to being led. Much of the work of self-development is to correct our relationship with the Sage by allowing ourselves to be led.

Anyone who works with the *I Ching,* whether he uses it for purposes of self-development or for guidance in money matters, or for the most mundane-seeming things, is being taught 'the way of the Sage', for no matter what our concern is, to achieve progress requires a realignment in our attitude to the cosmic point of view; this realignment moves us one more small step towards understanding the higher realities. Ultimately we are working on our spiritual nature. As the *I Ching* says, the Sage knows how to make use of everything.

In self-development we are guided in three main areas of action. Our primary goal seems to be that of correcting defective relationships, for these problems have been the main reason for consulting the *I Ching* as a source of help. Without our being aware of it, to attain this help we must form a partnership with the Sage, which requires changes on our part. We must "work on what has been spoiled" in terms of defective or decadent points of view. In correcting them we invoke the Creative Power; we enable it to work through us. The new relationships we form are founded on enduring principles. The three areas of action—correcting defective relationships, founding new ones on enduring principles, and invoking the power of the Creative, are the subject of many hexagrams and lines.

When the *I Ching* speaks of goals, it invariably refers to achieving human unity on an enduring basis. When the word "success" is mentioned, it refers to our general progress

103

toward this universal human goal. The following hexagrams define the essential principles of human unity: *Fellowship with Men, Coming to Meet, Gathering Together, The Family, Holding Together, Following, Influence, The Wanderer,* and *Progress.*

Coming to Meet (44) describes a correct relationship as one in which two people come to meet each other halfway. Halfway means that both are open and receptive to each other. *Youthful Folly* (4), which partly concerns the way we relate to the Sage, tells us that we need to have a childlike openness of mind, free of preconceptions and fixed opinions. The kind of action required, on receiving this hexagram, is to free ourselves of the impediments in our attitude that prevent our being open and receptive, or coming halfway to meet the Sage. The word "action" often refers to perfecting our attitude, giving up defenses and fixed positions, yielding on points of pride, or dispensing with inferiors which cause restlessness. In *Coming to Meet* the commentary also says that "the coming together must be free of dishonest ulterior motives, otherwise harm will result." This refers either to the way we relate to the Sage or to the way another person relates to us. As the Sage cannot respond to our ulterior purposes, we should take care not to respond to the ulterior motives of others.

To secure the support of the Sage it is necessary to attain innocence of mind. When we seek the Sage's help for selfish purposes we may receive the second line of Innocence (25) which reminds us not to anticipate the harvest while plowing; our incidental goals will be achieved as a natural consequence of following the path of the good for its own sake. Indeed, we prevent the things we seek from happening by attaching ourselves to having them. The things we seek cannot meet us halfway because we do not allow them to come on their own. The action counseled by this hexagram is to detach from our desires and ambitions; by attaining mental innocence, everything appropriate will be able to step toward us.

Coming to meet halfway also must be mutually voluntary, based on the principle of spontaneous attraction described in *The Marrying Maiden* (54) as the "essential principle of relatedness." We must maintain reserve in our relationships until the coming to meet is mutual. Maintaining reserve is the correct action (or non-action). Coming to meet halfway is possible only between people who are mutually honest and sincere in their way of life, so that they do not overstep the limits imposed by justice and equality. It is the great joy of such relationships that they are full of mutual trust and sensitivity.

We understand 'coming to meet' better if we compare it to a contract made between two people. If one is indolent in performing his part, or has mental reservations about what he is willing to do, the contract may fail. Although such a person may have entered the contract without any immediate objections, his attitude may contain objections which arise only at the time his obligations are to be performed. These hidden objections are what the *I Ching* calls "secret reservations of attitude." Such a person may secretly feel that contracts are not to be taken seriously; or, on seeing how difficult it is to fulfill his part, he may hedge on doing it because of some idea that all contracts are subject to fitting into his concept of what is "reasonable." In any case, it is impossible to come to meet such a person halfway, and the *I Ching* repeatedly advises us that it is better for us to go on our way alone and to wait until the fundamentals of unity are firmly established before we commit ourselves to other people. For a long time during our self-development we hedge on our commitment to following the path of the good for its own sake. Mentally we agree only to follow conditionally; if the going looks very difficult, our inferiors complain that they did not agree to follow under "these conditions." However, before we can be of true service to what is higher than ourselves, we must have developed firm loyalty to our principles.

This does not mean that we are intolerant or impatient with other people because they do not follow the path, any more than the Sage has been intolerant or impatient with us. If we recognize the source of evil in ourselves as being fear at the deepest level, how can we find any other cause for it in other people? Intolerance and impatience spring from our inferiors who desire things to be more comfortable, and who secretly doubt the path as the means by which we may be defended and by which we may correct defective relationships and injustices.

If we are already involved in defective relationships,

105

these become the means by which we learn the 'way of the Sage'. In correcting them we learn the true power of modesty as a shield and sword. For instance, we keep the inferiors in other people in check by perseveringly maintaining a proper distance and decorum, keeping disengaged from 'looking at' their behavior. When this produces a change in them so that they begin to relate to us sincerely, it is our duty to "meet them halfway," because at this time we are relating to their superior self; however, we are careful not to let go of our reserve to "enjoy" the improved situation. To do so is to endanger what one has gained through careful discipline. As *Grace* (22) says, "One is under the spell of grace and the mellow mood induced by wine. This grace can adorn, but it can also swamp us. Hence the warning not to sink into convivial indolence but to remain constant in perseverance. Good fortune depends on this." *Possession in Great Measure* (14) reaffirms this point in warning us that "benevolence alone is not sufficient at the time of *Possession in Great Measure,* for insolence might begin to spread. Insolence must be kept in bounds by dignity; then good fortune is assured." It is important to realize that in relating to people in this way, their superior self will emerge and disappear as their inferior man regains confidence; when their inferior man returns, we must immediately disengage and go on our way in the inner mental sense. To remain involved tells us that our ego has re-awakened and come into the scene, wanting to manage things. When we allow this to happen, we lose the Sage's help, but only until we regain self-discipline and free ourselves from the hold of our ego. This coming and going, apart from any role we may play in it, is natural. The hexagram *Abundance* (55) describes our short period of influence in the first line; in succeeding lines open receptivity is replaced by suspicion and mistrust; the analogy is given of a gradual eclipse of the sun and there is nothing we can do about it; we simply have to let it happen. But if we hold steadfastly to the power of truth, to what we know is correct, and humbly withdraw and disengage, the eclipse soon passes and once more we have an influence for the good. The hexagram warns, however, that we need to remain detached and cautious, relating to the person only as the moment allows, and avoiding any enthusiasm on our part. This swift re-emergence of the moment of influence is brought about by the Creative Power, in response to our correct attitude.

Fellowship with Men (13) also speaks of "secret reservations of attitude," but more in the context of factionalism. Whenever we set ourselves apart as different, better, or more deserving than others we create a barrier between ourselves and them that prevents their coming to meet us halfway. We do this when, as parents, we assume the right to abuse our children, or when, as teachers, we make our pupils feel less important than ourselves, or when, because we own something, we think that ownership gives us the right to degrade the essential dignity of anyone else. Other sorts of factionalism exist as well. For instance, when we make a faction with our inferiors to do something we know is incorrect, we exclude the Sage. Factionalism may be to agree with someone just to get along with him when we would better preserve our dignity by withholding our consent. Similarly, when we cater to another person's ego because it is uncomfortable to go on our way alone, we choose the high road of comfort rather than the low road of modesty and loneliness. Withdrawal from the high road is the action often counseled by the *I Ching*. The second and third lines of *Following* (17) speak of following the "baby" in ourselves which whines and cries, wanting this or that, or following the great man in ourselves. When we follow the latter, withdrawing from the baby, we experience a certain sense of loss as we give up the old comforts, but we find what we need "for the development of [our] personality," and in our hearts we feel satisfied.

Inner withdrawal is an action of perseverance that has its own reward, but only when it is a modest perseverance, not an attempt to impress others by getting them to notice our withdrawal. It is only a private withdrawal that preserves our purity of mind and our innocence, and which keeps us in the correct relationship to the Sage. In all instances when we receive the hexagram *Fellowship with Men* (13), we need to review our inmost thoughts to see if we harbor any kind of factionalism that would separate us from others or from the Sage. Feelings of alienation or vindictiveness separate us from others, and clinging to such impurities of thought separate us from the Sage.

Disengagement from negative images arouses the power

107

of the Creative to solve problems in a just and correct manner. Such negative images may be feelings of alienation and hostility, doubts about our path and its outcome, or anxieties caused by fear; these images, in turn, cause us to desire to make the situation different, or to ambitiously seek swift progress, or to decisively take matters in hand to bring about a "solution" to the problem. The fifth line of *Conflict* (6) says that we may safely turn the matter over to the Sage to be resolved by itself. In many situations the problem is resolved, not through any external action that arises spontaneously on our part, but by simply "letting it happen," through letting go of the problem. Our "action" is to "let go." This is what the judgment in *Biting Through* (21) means when it advises us to "let justice be administered." In effect, we turn it over to the higher power to administer. In practicing disengagement from negative images and their offspring emotions, we train ourselves not to brand adverse situations as "bad." By not deciding the situation is "unfavorable," we remain open to learning something from it, and allow the hidden force to resolve the difficulties in a favorable way. From the *I Ching* point of view, adversity provides the opportunity for inner growth and development as we overcome the doubts, anxieties and judgments that block our access to the Creative Power. It is also its view that all evil, either in us or in other people, arises from doubts and misunderstandings. Doubting that we, in and of ourselves, are sufficiently equipped to succeed in life, we develop a false image, or ego. Doubting that we have help from the Creative, we fear what life has to offer, therefore build defenses against the unknown. Misunderstanding Fate, we believe that we are assaulted, from time to time, by an evil force. All these doubts and misunderstandings are at the root of how people relate incorrectly to each other.

In the foregoing examples we have seen that action tends to be expressed in terms of applying limits to our thoughts and actions. Accepting such self-imposed limits is the message of *Limitation* (60). We are counseled by this hexagram to rehearse our limits before we become involved in trying situations. By doing this we are prepared to withstand the dangers and threats which such situations present. *Limitation* also informs us that if we would set limits on the behavior of others, we must first limit ourselves. If we would cure another person's hostility toward us—which is a form of self-defense—we must free ourselves first of any feelings of alienation we may have towards him. This alienation may exist in any factional attitude we have towards him, such as feeling he is hopeless, or impossible to influence. Another necessary limitation we must place on ourselves is that of restraining ourselves, through self-discipline, from expecting quick results. Our inferiors impatiently measure the other person's behavior to see if we are having an effect. The *I Ching* explains that we must learn to work with time as the vehicle of the Creative Force. Working with time, adapting to the fact that slow progress is the only progress that endures, is part of the process of non-action. We need to withdraw from impatience and "flow," as with water that only runs downhill. We need to prohibit our inferiors from "watching the team horse," and from putting images of gloom and doom before our inner eye. Sometimes doing these things requires what can only be called "galling limitation," and "sublime perseverance," but it is only by such means that we can gain superiority over our recalcitrant inferiors. We also find that during such times we can overcome the assaults of our inferiors if we mount a resolute determination to withstand them; they can withstand such resoluteness on our part for a maximum time of about three minutes, then they collapse. It is important to remember that they are but paper dragons and they do not have the invincible power they make us think they have. It is also important to remember that when we cling steadfastly to our path, we also get help from the Creative, but even more readily if we remember to ask for help.

Perfecting our inner nature in the ways described develops the power of inner truth. Being firm in our minds as to what is essential and correct is also a part of the power of inner truth. The hexagram *Revolution* (49) stresses that what we ask of people must "correspond with a higher truth and not spring from arbitrary or petty motives." Getting this line may indicate that we need to reflect on what we ask of people. What we think as consistent with the demands of justice may not be so from the cosmic point of view. We may have imagined, for example, that a person who has been unfair with us ought to go through a series of steps to re-establish their

109

credibility and good will. In effect, we are saying that we require them to meet conditions of our specifications, otherwise the injustice cannot be erased. Such demands are the work of our self-righteous pride and ego. The way in which a person returns to the path is not properly our business; furthermore, when they have returned, we must meet them halfway. We also need to avoid using the moment to gain recognition that we were "right." In all situations our progress is attained through the help of the creative; our partnership with the Sage is based on our coming to meet him with a pure mind, which arouses his help to correct the situation. If we then forget our responsibility to this power, or appropriate the success to our personal ends, breakthrough and breakdown occurs, as the hexagram *Break-through/Resoluteness* (43) makes clear.

While we are prevented, by our limits, from telling other people what to do, we can say what we are willing to do or not do in following our path. To respond only from firmly placed values as to what is just and correct is to act from inner truth. As it says in the hexagram *Conflict* (6), if we take everything "into consideration at the very beginning" and define our rights and duties, "the cause of conflict is removed in advance." This is possible only if we have come to the realization of exactly what is correct, and if we are unwilling to depart from the path. People intuit our point of view. If we are hesitant or tentative about what we are willing to do, or have no limits, people will constantly overstep the boundaries of correctness and place us in untenable positions.

The power of inner truth is directly diminished by doubt. The first line of *Gathering Together* (45) says, "If you are sincere, but not to the end, there will sometimes be confusion, sometimes gathering together." Where we waver, others waver. The power of negative thought, we need to remember, is actively destructive, not quiescent. In the hexagram *Breakthrough (Resoluteness)* (43) it is said that even "one inferior man" occupying "a ruling position" is "able to oppress superior men." If we have increased our prices, then worry that people might stop buying, they feel our doubt and hesitate to buy. There is a saying in Taoism that "fear is the place where harm enters."

If we have vacillated for years and suddenly cease doing

110

so, we may not expect people to change their habitual view of us quickly. They will still expect us to vacillate and be weak and continue to relate to us in an indolent manner until our new attitude gradually penetrates through to them. This slow process of penetration requires us to be patient and persevering.

The action described thus far—that of non-action, of keeping our inner attitude correct, works through the power of inner truth. Inner truth has to mount to great strength before it can break through obdurate situations. It mounts in strength in direct proportion to our inner perseverance and will-power to hold to the correct path, and it acts on the principle of gentle penetration described in *The Gentle (The Penetrating, Wind)* (57). Just as roots penetrate rocks and break them apart, perseverance in the correct attitude breaks through closed minds. The action is best described as the dawning of light. It is very gradual. In such a manner do we experience the awakening of our understanding in our everyday lessons with the *I Ching*.

A second type of action arises spontaneously out of a correct attitude. This action manifests itself as a response to what is happening, and although we realize we are acting, we do so with such detachment that we feel we are observers rather than doers; the action happens through us, rather than by us. We are conduits for what arises in the hidden world. Sometimes this action is very forceful and abrupt, and so different from our normal perseverance in non-action that it takes us completely by surprise; moreover, we may even think that what we did was beyond our limits, but in asking the *I Ching* afterwards, it is confirmed that the action was correct. We are aware that it had the correct effect and was appropriate, and that we could not have planned it. Sometimes the action taken is a very quiet, calming action, but again, we are detached. Such moments do not come often, but usually happen in difficult situations in which the help of the Creative is greatly needed.

Such spontaneous action can only occur when we are in a receptive and open state of mind. It may take place after we have been misunderstood and challenged by other people's inferiors, and have strictly held to our limits. Suddenly we say or do the correct thing. Steadfastness has aroused the Creative Power to act through us. The state of mind in which such action can take place is that of emptiness. We have mentally disengaged from any intentions or plans, any feelings of urgency or alienation, of wanting to do or dreading to do anything about the situation at hand. We have also become free of any discouraging feelings of helplessness, and have allowed ourselves to be dependent upon the cosmos to let things work out as they will. In arriving at this "empty place," the place of no thought, or what in Zen is called "no mind," we are in tune with the Creative.

Inner correctness also activates what the *I Ching* calls "the helpers"—those hidden and often suppressed great and good elements in other people that, once aroused, provide the necessary inner assent to accomplish needed changes. The lines in the *I Ching* that call for "seeing the great man" and "holding to the great man" mean that we need to hold to the possibility of these elements in others, even though the most unpleasant elements are visible. If it is impossible to conceive of the great man in another person, it is sufficient to disperse or disengage from our negative feelings about him; to be neutral in attitude is to automatically remain open to their potential goodness. In this manner the Sage disengages from us when we leave the path of modesty and conscientiousness, and leaves us to our own devices.

Similar to this spontaneous action is a slow building action that steadily mounts in intensity to a denouement that just happens by itself. This action is described in the lines of *The Taming Power of the Great* (26). Relating properly to the situation in which it occurs is described in *Preponderance of the Small* (62). Complex, unseen movements are taking place. We may be warned by receiving the first line of *The Creative* (1) that unseen factors are at work and that we ought not to make any external moves on our part. *Preponderance of the Great* (28) may also warn us that we are in an "exceptional time" in which it is possible to make great strides forward, or, if we are careless, the time of opportunity may pass us by. During this time the external situation seems to demand our taking some action, but we don't know what action. As *Preponderance of the Small* tells us, it is necessary to wait in the 'ambiguous spot', doing nothing. Doing nothing and waiting in the correct attitude results in a build-up of inner power. The taming and holding onto this power is the subject of *The Taming Power of the Great* (26), which speaks of daily self-renewal through keeping still as the only means of remaining at the peak of our inner powers. In "taming" this power by resisting the urge to act, we experience a sense of discomfort. Waiting in the ambiguous spot is galling to our inferiors who point to the "threatening dangers of non-action." The rush of desire to do something is pictured as a bull's horns and a rhinocerus's tusk, which may be controlled through seeing with clarity that it is not yet time to act. Finally, with our being hardly aware of it, the inner power has its effect and the obstacles are overcome. When this happens we get the top line, which says, "He attains the way of heaven, success." Through waiting and controlling our inner energy, inner power grew and the victory was won. It was as if the root inside the boulder swelled and split the boulder apart. At this final moment those who were hostile or unreceptive change and became open to us. This change is dramatic and inexplicable, outside the boundaries of any logical process.

Waiting in the ambiguous spot involves risks and dangers which must be overcome if we are to succeed. *The Abysmal (Danger)* (29) refers to the danger which may cause us to abandon our path if we entertain even the slightest doubt. Doubt may cause us to make some move to solve the problem; for example, we may give up on ourselves, or on others, or on the Creative. These moves cause us to lose our partnership with the Sage, and because they are also against our inner nature, they result in darkening our inner light. Once we overcome this first level of danger we encounter threats on a second level. We may feel alienated towards those who made us "suffer through such trying situations," as our inferiors would put it, or the pressure of the situation may cause us to fall into conflict with others. Having conquered these risks we may receive the fifth line in *Before Completion* (64) which confirms our having persevered through the situation to the end: "Perseverance brings good fortune. No remorse. The light of the superior man is true. Good fortune."

The sort of patience in waiting referred to in the *I Ching* is a unique focusing of will to hold to what is good in ourselves, in other people, and in the life process, so that the inferior man, wherever he exists, is overthrown. First we retreat from any inferior impulses we have; then we disengage

113

our attention from the other person, leaving it truly up to him to do or not do the right thing. This kind of humble acceptance, in which we "cling to the power of truth," arouses the Creative Power. We do not need to like the person, or to believe in him, or to believe in our own power—quite the opposite; truly, we are powerless. Without going from the extreme of disbelief to the extreme of belief, we simply relinquish, or sacrifice our disbelief. In sacrificing it, we return to the mean, the empty place, the neutral place, the place of the Creative. In so doing we retain our inner dignity and we preserve theirs; by recognizing and accepting our own powerlessness we give them the space to find themselves. This space acts as a kind of cosmic mirror in which the other person perceives and apprehends his inferior man. In this manner we make it possible for another person's superior man to regain control.

The build-up of inner power depends upon the self-limitation described. We also need to be aware of the kinds of things that damage our inner power. When the situation momentarily improves we tend to become careless, forgetting our limits; small mistakes, such as entertaining petty or unworthy thoughts, or engaging in fantasies, diminish inner power. Doubts on the other hand, totally collapse it. Clearly, inner power is acquired through voluntarily placing upon ourselves the strictest limits of restraint, humility, and perseverance in correct inner thoughts. To maintain this power requires that we control both ambition and the tendency to relax into careless self-confidence. Inner power is maintained through daily self-renewal—letting go of everything and keeping still every day. At the same time, it is impossible to free ourselves from entrenched habits of mind all at once. Knowing what we must do, we put all our will toward it and march forward with great determination and ambition. The goals, however, may only be achieved through a gradual, step by step process which includes both effort and failure. We need to forgive ourselves for not always living up to our standards, and for frequently failing. It is unreasonable to expect too much, too soon, therefore the *I Ching* says we must put "limitation, even upon limitation."

Modesty as a Shield and a Sword

In using the *I Ching* for guidance in difficult situations over a period of years, we not only come to understand how modesty brings about our defense and furtherance, but how it also acts as a tool for rectifying our relationships.

If a person is treating us presumptuously, as in leaving his dirty dishes for us to clean, and if we remind him of this, he may correct his habits for a few days, but gradually revert to the same pattern of neglect. This he does from egotistical indolence—something in his point of view makes him feel he has the right to be indifferent. If we were to have such an attitude toward the Sage, the Sage would withdraw the feeling of his presence, leaving us in the emptiness of the void. Likewise, we must withdraw from the indolent person, "cutting our inner strings" of attachment to them, and no longer look at their wrong-doings with our inner eye. This enables the person to see what he is doing in the mirror created by the void. By dispersing any alienation we may feel, we also lend strength to his superior self. Momentarily, his ego is overcome. We need to realize that this change is short-lived, but it is an essential beginning. The change does not last because it is only founded on his response to feeling the void. It becomes a permanent change when he sees clearly that unity with others depends upon his devoting himself to correcting his mistakes. Only then can we abandon a more formal way of relating to him.

The sense of loss, loneliness, or poverty of self a person feels on our withdrawing from him is what, in *Biting Through* (21), is called "punishment." The punishment works only if it is applied in the way described in the lines of this hexagram. These lines make clear that on encountering the ego of another person, we must consistently and immediately withdraw, neither contending with him nor trying to force progress by leverage. We withdraw, accepting his state of mind, letting him go. We must take care not to withdraw with any other attitude than that required to maintain inner serenity, and to keep from giving up on him. If we withdraw with feelings of alienation, or of self-righteousness, our ego is involved as the punisher. The ego, as the third line of this hexagram says, "lacks the power and authority" to punish. The

115

culprits not only do not submit, but "by taking up the problem the punisher arouses poisonous hatred against himself." One person's ego may not punish another person's ego.

Withdrawal as punishment will help us correct spoiled relationships only if we consistently apply its principles. It is somewhat like training animals by positive and negative reinforcement. When an animal misbehaves we restrain it and convey our disapproval; when a person misbehaves, we convey a subconscious message by inwardly withdrawing; when an animal performs its lessons well, we unfailingly pat it; when a person returns to the path of responding correctly, we likewise go to meet him halfway, rather than tell him he is doing things correctly. In this way he comes to relating correctly from his own need to relate correctly and we do not force it on him. Our consistency and discipline in feeling out each moment and responding to it does the work. It is unnecessary to watch a person's behavior to see if he is becoming worse or better; we need only be in tune with ourselves. Our inner voice warns us precisely when to withdraw and when to relate. We need only listen within.

It is an important *I Ching* principle to work with a situation only so long as the other person is receptive and open, and to retreat the instant this receptivity wanes. The hexagram *Abundance* (55) describes the coming and going of this moment of influence as a gradual eclipse of the sun. The first line pictures a time of influence, in which people who are open and receptive to each other "can be together ten days, and it is not a mistake," although in actual time it may mean only five minutes. The second line pictures the beginning of an eclipse; suspicion and mistrust begin to obscure the light. This changes to a total eclipse in the third line, when no influence is possible. "It is as though his right arm were broken," and "the most insignificant persons have pushed themselves into the foreground." (These persons symbolize inferior thoughts.) In the next line the eclipse is passing and once more an opening occurs in which we may have an influence. When we understand that this represents a natural cycle of influence, we learn to "let go" when the moment of influence passes, and not to press our views. This gives other people the space they need to move away from us and return of their own accord. The Sage relates to us in precisely this manner, and the hexagram comments that the Sage is never sad, in view of our coming and going, but is always like the sun at mid-day. In the same way we must avoid egotistical enthusiasm when we think we are making progress, or become discouraged when the dark period ensues. Throughout the cycle we learn to remain detached, holding steadily to the light within us and within others. The instant we strive to influence, we "push upward blindly." If we insist on accomplishing the goal at all costs, our inner light is darkened and our will to see things through, is damaged. It is important to preserve our personality from the kind of effort that damages our will.

The fifth line in *Biting Through* additionally warns us of the danger posed by our natural tendency to be lenient the instant a person begins to improve. We must be hesitant, skipping no steps, and "make every effort to be like yellow gold—that is, as true as gold and as impartial as yellow." To fall victim to careless enthusiasm because of our desire to enjoy the improved situation is to appropriate the results of our work to our selfish ends. As long as we remain conscious of this danger we will escape being trapped by it.

When we recognize another person's ego, their ego and the inferiors it commands, feel affirmed and supported; when we withdraw that recognition, their ego and the accompanying inferiors feel abandoned. When the ego fails, in this manner, to provide the inferiors with the happiness it has promised, the inferiors lose confidence in it. They then turn back to the superior self for guidance, but the superior self is too weak to maintain control for long against the inferiors' habitual ideas of what the personality needs to succeed. If we too readily restore the inferiors' sense of comfort, they conclude that they have misread the seriousness of the situation and return their loyalties to the ego.

The strength of a person's ego corresponds to the amount of attention it can attract. On the most simple level this recognition is by eye-to-eye contact; on the more basic inner level we strengthen other people's egos by watching them with our inner eye. If we are annoyed with someone, we are watching him with our inner eye. Only when we withdraw both our eye-to-eye contact and our inner gaze do we deprive his ego of its power. An *I Ching* line says "We cannot lead those whom we follow." By following them with our inner

117

eye we do not walk our own path but attend to theirs. This not only gratifies their ego, but if we see this situation in meditation, it is as if we are attached to them by hidden underground cables which must be cut. It is as if we are acting as a lifeguard who is watching to save them from themselves. As long as they recognize that someone is going to save them, they carelessly begin to swim with the sharks. They do this not only because they feel a false sense of security, but because it guarantees that we pay attention to them. As long as we play the role of lifeguard, the person we care about will not save himself; for his own good it is necessary to withdraw, cut our inner strings and leave matters up to him; this is also to cease doubting him.

Very often our withdrawal is challenged—the other person will try to get some response from us. This challenge occurs because our adherence to duty has inspired a certain envy. The envy may first be expressed as hatred. The *I Ching* says, however, that "we can endure the dislike of others." Hatred failing, we may next experience envy as a flattering admiration. At first our inner strength and inner power are interpreted as a mask—one that people would like to possess; it is as if we embody the image of what they would like to be; to discover whether it is real or just a mask, they test us. These envious assaults are called "wars." Modesty, again, is our defense: we conscientiously search for the right way to respond. As long as we are sincere the right way shows itself at the right time. Meanwhile, we prepare for these wars by firming our inner discipline and readying our minds to hold to the empty place. In the second line of *The Ting* (50) it is written "My comrades are envious, but they cannot harm me." The commentary says, "If a man concentrates on real undertakings, he may indeed experience envy and disfavor, but that is not dangerous. The more he limits himself to his actual achievement, the less harm can the envious inflict on him." We do not allow ourselves to be drawn, in any discussions, off the pinpoint and core of what is essential, but rigorously maintain our innocence and purity of mind.

In meditation I saw three images which symbolized the assault of the envious ego. The first was that of a dragon, gaudy and flood-lit, staring at me with fierce eyes, blowing fire and smoke. My impulse was to flee, but a voice said,

"Stay! Look at it," giving me the courage to do so. I saw that the dragon was surprised that I was still there. It snorted and roared again, then looked to see if I was frightened. When I was not, it lost all its power. As I realized that its bravado was nothing but a charade, it began to crumble and go up in smoke like the Wicked Witch of the West in the *Wizard of Oz*. It was only a paper dragon. As I pondered this, another image appeared. I saw a cat hitting a mouse until it became unconscious. When the mouse regained consciousness, the cat hit it again until it ceased to move. I noted that the cat was interested in the mouse only when the mouse was active. Next I saw a snake coiled around a tree which had a nest with two birds in it. One of the two birds was terrorized by the snake while the other was indifferent to it. The snake, I noted, was interested only in the terrorized bird and ignored the other one. These threee images represented aspects of the ego as a predatory creature which seeks only to disturb those things it can bully or from which it can get a reaction. When we fail to react, either with fear in the case of the dragon or snake, or with conscious attention, as in the case of the cat, it leaves us alone.

Another meditation showed the nature of the ego when it is involved in unreasoning anger. This time a bull charged toward me, but I noticed that I was in a bull-fighting ring with a red cape in my hands. By holding out the cape as a bull fighter would do, it only thought it was engaging me as it gored the cape. I realized that to ignore someone who is angry only makes him more angry. It is possible, however, to react without reacting by replying in a vague and not too sensible way—to hold out a cape, so to speak. An angry person is not interested in being reasonable; any reply we make is misunderstood. One that makes no sense has the advantage of satisfying the person demanding a response, gives him nothing further to argue about, and helps us remain unengaged. Determination on our part to keep from engaging in conflict brings the help of the Sage so that we say the correct thing.

Still another meditation image came to me on the danger of idle curiosity. In this meditation I had walked into a snake's territory and it coiled back to strike me. I realized that by intruding into its territory, it, being a shy and defensive

119

creature, naturally sprang to defend itself. If we insist on threatening another person by interfering in his affairs through idle curiosity, we endanger ourselves. Idle curiosity is also against the Cosmic Law.

The best defense against evil is to allow ourselves to be aware of it without stopping to stare at it and brand it. We notice it only peripherally and keep it at arm's length so as not to become infected by it. (To be affected by it is also to become infected by it.) A line in the *I Ching* counsels us to walk in the midst of danger as if it did not exit. This keeps evil at bay. By seeing and knowing evil, we do not see or know evil. The novel, *Little Lord Fauntleroy,* was an example of the way not to see evil. The grandson, young Lord Fauntleroy, simply misinterpreted all the old Lord Fauntleroy's inferior comments and motives, making them, by slight shifts of emphasis, into the highest motives; eventually, the old Lord began to want to live up to this best view of himself that his grandson held. This is not to say that the way of the *I Ching* is to memorize such an approach; everyone must find his own way of keeping evil at bay so as to walk in the midst of danger as if it did not exist.

If we find the way of the Sage difficult, the *I Ching* counsels us to remember the *ancestors*—those human beings who "went before us" on this inner journey, developing themselves and persevering through the difficulties. They had no more will power than we have, yet they overcame the difficulties. When we follow the path of the good and the beautiful we get the help we need from the Creative Power. In yielding our self-defenses we are defended; in relinquishing our wants, we have all that we need; in limiting ourselves, the Creative Power is aroused to do the work. Through following our path and coming to meet the Sage halfway, life becomes a constant receiving of gifts.

Although we have limits and guidelines, there are no rules. Making rules and then relying on them is to turn things over to our inferiors. The inferior man would reduce truth to a set of rules in order to force others to conform by leverage; or he would say there are no rules in order to have license to break inner laws. The Tao may not be defined, only approximated. Lao Tzu said, "Man follows the way of the Earth, The Earth follows the ways of Heaven, Heaven follows the

120

way of Tao, Tao follows its own ways." By listening within
and following the guidance of the hexagrams, we may follow
the ways of Tao and "attain the way of heaven. Success."

The Creative Experience

It is the nature of the Creative to 'further', as the first
hexagram, *The Creative* states. Furthering can occur on many
levels. When, on consulting the *I Ching* for the first time and
it replies that if we relate properly we will be furthered, we
interpret this to mean that our goals will be attained, or great
strides of progress will be made. Our hopes and expectations,
being high, cause us to overlook the simpler everyday meaning: the first step toward any goal is to see with clarity what
must be done. When we get the hexagram *The Creative,* it
may refer to having attained clarity; we understand the way
of the Sage, by which all difficult things may be achieved.

Furthering most often refers to comprehending, for
when we see that the way of the Sage is truly a superior way,
and when we see with inner knowing how well it mounts the
steps upwards to success, we need not muster up so much
strength to persevere. Clarity gives us strength to wait, for in
the superior view by which we see the scheme of things, am-
biguity disappears, with all its threats. Clarity *is* strength; giving us a superior view is the first means by which the Sage
helps us. Having a superior viewpoint is the difference between seeing a garden at ground level, where no semblance of
order is visible, and seeing the garden from a sufficient height
whereby the orderliness of the rows becomes visible.

We find that furthering—the advancement of our point
of view—occurs in steps. Furthering advances us to the next
step in knowledge, or the next step in invention; on the
spiritual level, it is an advancement to the next step in our
perception of the Cosmic Order. The pianist learns a new and
better way of playing a passage; he "stumbles" across it. The
writer knows something needs to be expressed, but he has no
grasp of how to say it; the image comes to him quite suddenly, when his mind is on other things. The artist is muddled
about a section of his painting; suddenly the color or form
comes to him; the inventor, likewise, gets a breakthrough
which enables him to complete his invention. In all of these

121

situations, furthering, as the Creative Experience, has occurred; it has come as a breakthrough—a sudden perception. Sometimes we see a series of images or a mental schematic. Sometimes we understand without being aware of seeing or hearing anything—the answer seems to well up from below, or enter our heads from above as if there is a special hole through which it comes. We experience it differently at different times, and each of us experiences it in different ways, but always, it is in the form of receiving. Once it begins, we let it happen and keep open to it, for we know that if we interfere, we will lose our connection with it, and it will cease.

If the Creative Experience happens in visual form, what we see is a Cosmic Picture. It has a lot of detail, each bit of which is part of the answer we seek. Once, I was asked to attend a Quaker Meeting at which I was to talk informally on the *I Ching* after the customary one hour period of silence. Because of the informal nature of the talk I could not see how I would be able to present the *I Ching* in the orderly sequence of ideas I thought to be essential, if those present were not to be confused. During the hour of meditation I saw two images. First I saw the image of a string, such as one of the large strings on a bass viol, suspended from the ceiling to the floor; a hand plucked it vigorously. Then I saw that every person in the room had come with pre-occupations which separated them from one another. As the string vibrated, their schisms simply vibrated away. Thereafter, the room contained only a feeling of oneness among us. The second image was that of a schematic consisting of a horizontal line that had a plus sign at one end and a negative sign at the other; a small point designated the center of the line. Everything above the line represented the external world and everything below, the inner world. I saw that at the beginning of my study of the *I Ching* my "outer world location" was at the negative end of the line and completely above the line. My only reality was the outer world; moreover, my means for dealing with the outer world had ceased to work; the only place of safety, although I hardly recognized its existence, was the inner world. My new location on the schematic was shifted to the under side of the line at the extreme positive end. This new location represented the fact that I had no choice but to dwell in the inner world until I fully recognized how the inner world affected my outer world existence. Eventually, I came back to the center of the line, with half of me above and half below the line, in a state of balance between both. This schematic represented what happens when we use the *I Ching* for self-development; it represented what happened to me and was given with the message, "cling to the schematic." In the free-flowing talk that followed, I was able to use people's questions as departure-points for referring to the schematic and my own experience of being taught by the *I Ching*. In this way the talk had an orderly progression and unity that would not otherwise have been possible. Moreoever, the questions seemed veritably designed to allow me to follow the schematic. This was a typical Creative Experience.

An ancient Chinese commentator on the *I Ching* said that if we want to understand the meaning of a hexagram we must follow the images it presents as one follows a hare. The images spark a thought process in our minds which may be "followed" in this manner. We do not interfere with the process, merely follow it; but if our thoughts go so far as to lose sight of the original images, he said, we go too far. The Creative Experience begins in a similar manner—something is sparked, and we follow it without interfering; our intellect may serve to remember it, or write it down and otherwise bring it to fruition, but in every case, our intellect remains as servant and follower, not leader.

All of us has experienced the Creative in some way or another. We have done so when we were in a particular state of mind. We come upon this state accidentally and like Alice falling into the hole, forget how we got there. The *I Ching,* through the hexagrams, develops our awareness of the doorway to the state, and of the rules surrounding our use of the Creative Product, for there are definite Cosmic Laws governing our use of it.

In order to have access to the Creative Experience there must first be a need to know. Secondly, we must acknowledge our need and that we don't, in and of ourselves, know the answer, and that we can't, in and of ourselves, find it. The sooner we acknowledge these humble beginnings, the sooner we will make the Creative Experience available to us. As long as we think we "do it" or that there is some trick to getting there, the doorway will remain closed. The sooner we recognize that it is a gift from the Creative, the sooner the doorway will open for us. Simplicity and humility are the beginnings of the Creative Experience, and asking for help is the key. Next, what we seek must be unselfish; the musician seeks to express the eternal genius of the music; the inventor sees that his invention will benefit many people; the writer sees that his work will help others attain insight into the problems of their own lives; all this is to say that the person believes in the value of what he is doing. As Lao Tsu said, the master potter makes the pot for its own sake. That is enough. But if a person's mind is beclouded with images of his success or fame, the Creative Door will not open.

Contemplation is the effort to see, to bring into conscious focus the connections between our external experience and its origins in the image world. If we understand the underlying image, we understand the thing. We see it (in a flash) in its cosmic placement, or hierarchy, and in its relationship to other things. This need to see, to solve a particular problem, exists as a sort of *coan*, or Cosmic Puzzle. It is our nature to solve these puzzles, for through coming into contact with the Creative, we learn about our spiritual nature and the meaning of life. *Coans* are part of the inner growth process by which we bring into being our spiritual existence. For this reason, in Zen, it is said that one learns Zen not through studying Zen, but by studying archery or flower arrangements, or things that challenge one to solve a problem. The problem is inherently cosmic in nature, requiring that we come into the proper relationship with the Creative to obtain its solution.

Imagination, or our attempt to hypothetically construct the answer, is our ego's attempt to mastermind the problem. It is part of the Cosmic Humor that we struggle fruitlessly by repeated imaginative and intellectual assaults upon the *coan*. It is only when we let go, sighing, "I just can't do it, it isn't in my power," that suddenly it comes freely as a gift. Unfortunately, we gradually begin to think that the idea was "ours," and forget where it came from. As the fourth line of *Inner Truth* (61) says, "The moon nearly at the full. The team horse goes astray." Here, in our partnership with the Creative, we stand as the moon in relation to the sun, reflecting the greater light. The commentary says that "at the moment when the moon becomes full and stands directly opposite the sun, it begins to wane." When we forget the source of enlightenment, we begin to lose it. When we first come into contact with the Creative we are undeveloped and do not know how to relate to it. We stumble upon it and for a time we steal the ideas, as the dwarf, Alberich stole the Rhinemaidens' gold. We need to lose the help of the Creative a number of times before we develop the humility to treat the Sage with tenderness and gratitude, and to free ourselves from the presumption that we create it all to our specification, which viewpoint the *I Ching* calls, "Contemplation through the crack of the door."

I happened to read *Zen in the Art of Archery* by Eugen Herrigel and *Grist for the Mill* by Ram Dass simultaneously. I rarely read two books at once but on this occasion I was reading the former when a friend asked me to read the latter and give my opinion of it. In this way I happened to read the sections in which both Ram Dass and Eugen Herrigel experienced a breakthrough, at the same time. Doing so led to a breakthrough for me as well. Ram Dass had tried to mastermind the answer to his *coan* time and again while in the Zen monastery. Finally, he concluded that he could not find the answer; immediately, upon admitting this to himself, the answer came. Similarly, Eugen Herrigel had spent five years practicing the techniques that lead to "letting go of the bowstring without conscious thought," which challenge was his *coan*. Finally, in exasperation he gave up, also admitting that he "just couldn't do it." Instantly the string flew from his hand effortlessly, and the arrow hit its mark. The next day I played tennis as I never did before, with the awareness that I, in and of myself, can't do it, and that "it" does it. As long as I allowed "it" to make the shots without interference, my plays and responses were far beyond my customary level of ability. When I interfered, thinking it would "be better to go cross-court this time" or "down the line," my shots misfired. It was an amazing demonstration of this correct way of relating to the Creative, and of enabling the power of the Creative to work through us. We cannot achieve this connection with the Creative by will, but by attaining that particular state of mind. My wanting to win was an interference; feeling proud of a shot was an interference; engaging with my opponent's competitive ego by wanting to reply with a particularly good shot, was also an interference. Later, when I attempted to duplicate my relationship with the Creative in order to play as well again, my attempt failed. Nor could I outwit the Creative by adopting the attitude of "not caring whether I won or not." The Creative responds only to real humility, which, in tennis, is simply to play to the best of one's ability and to accept the ups and down of the game equally.

In "following," we find that the Creative leads us to do things we may never have thought to do. Only in retrospect do we realize that we were being prepared for something new. To give example, for five years I led a small *I Ching* discussion group in weekly meetings. Then one day I had a meditation in which I saw our group sitting in a train station which was far off on an unused spur of railroad track. "No one went there anymore," the voice in my meditation said. Then I saw a train station like that of Grand Central Station in New York City during the days when it was the center of the traveling world. I saw that I should go there—wherever "there" was. The meaning of this meditation did not become clear at once, but I began to feel, and get confirmation from my hexagrams, that I was supposed to be doing something else. Gradually it dawned on me that I was to make a book of my notes on the hexagrams. After four more years these were completed and were published as *A Guide to the I Ching*. Publishing was to be my Grand Central Station. It is in such a way that we are led to the tasks we are meant to do, and to the way in which we are supposed to do them.

Not only are we led to do things, we receive help we don't even know we need. When I began to write this chapter on the Creative Experience, I thought it would only be a small section because I had only a few pages of notes on the subject. Immediately, I was prevented from writing by other work that unexpectedly intervened. Meanwhile, I had meditations on the way we think and on aspects of the subject I had not previously experienced. I began to be aware that I was being helped and needed help I didn't know I needed. There were aspects of the Creative of which I was as yet unaware. Attaining the Creative Help is not necessarily based on our desire to know or the feeling that we need to know; rather, it is help given us to complete our work in the correct way, as the next step in our progress. Once we allow ourselves to stay in the proximity of the Creative—through being guided by the hexagrams and meditating—everything becomes easy and appropriate. Is this not another meaning of "the easy" implied in the *I*? Sometimes my meditations have told me to start writing and I would get the help as I went along. We cannot know how the Creative Experience is next going to show itself—it always happens on its own terms and in its own ways.

When we attain a close working relationship with the Creative we find that not only do the ideas come to us, but supporting material as well, if any is needed. Some years ago I experienced this phenomenon when I was working on a writing project that needed documentation. For months I kept receiving clippings from friends who knew I was working on this material; other friends would see books in libraries and bring them to me. This continuous help, coming from so many quarters, at the precise time I needed it, seemed very phenomenal to me at a time when I knew nothing (consciously) of the Creative.

The doorway that leads to the Creative Experience is that of modesty and acceptance. We wait patiently and allow ourselves to be guided. When the experience begins, we allow it to occur on its own terms; we follow it as we might follow the rabbit's trail. Then it happens because it is what we need, to go from here, as part of the life process and progress. It fits into the Tao—the direction in which the Divine Will is moving. The terms on which it comes are, that if it is to benefit us, it must also be of benefit through us, to all others. The hexagram *Increase* (42), which concerns our having this help, warns that "if great help comes to a man from on high, this increased strength must be used to achieve something great for which he might otherwise never have found energy, or readiness to take responsibility. Great good fortune is produced by selflessness, and in bringing about great good fortune, he remains free of reproach."

The Creative Experience cannot happen if we are indolent of mind, or if, caught in a pause in our progress, we don't want to go on, and we don't care. Our basic movement toward growth and light must not be shut down, or our inner light submerged. Doubts and negative thoughts must be

127

dispersed. The Creative Power will not operate when we are fixed in our views, or when we desire the Creative Experience to the point of trying to force it to happen. We must place ourselves in the mind of "letting it happen."

We shut off the Creative Experience if we consciously interfere with it. While meditating we may be instructed to respond to the meditation images in a certain way, but this differs from conscious interference or attempts to manipulate the flow of images. If, after we have had meditation experiences or have had the Creative Help in our work, we then appropriate the help for selfish purposes, our successes are inevitably followed by failure in the end. We may not manipulate or play with the Creative Power. The third line of *The Creative* (1) speaks on this point: "A sphere of influence opens up for the great man. His fame begins to spread. The masses flock to him. His inner power is adequate to the increased outer activity... But danger lurks here at the place of transition from lowliness to the heights. Many a great man has been ruined because the masses flocked to him and swept him into their course. Ambition has destroyed his integrity. However, true greatness is not impaired by temptations."

The Zen practice of "no mind" aims at putting oneself in the proximity of the Creative. "No mind" means to be free of intellect and to attain a conscious innocence and purity of mind. Putting ourselves in the proximity of the Creative means that we, like the concert violinist, by practicing, maximize our form so that the Creative has a medium through which to express itself. Although this partnership is a 50/50 one, our part requires a 100 percent devotion to our path if we are to keep in contact with it. Our daily practice is that of self-renewal through meditation. The writer must nurture his material as a hen broods eggs, staying in contact with it. The inventor must ponder his problem, and like the chicken, look at it from every angle. He must do this first in a detached way; then the Creative helps.

The Creative helps when it will—in the early morning, in the middle of the night, while we are gardening or driving our car. When it comes, it must be attended to at that moment, with ourselves and our attentiveness serving as midwife. If we fail to watch and listen carefully, or allow it to act on us totally, it goes by and never comes again in the same way. It is important to write, or draw, or otherwise utilize the products of our creative realizations.

We also find that the Creative Experience comes at the most appropriate times. For example, I was advising a group on publishing a history. During the morning on which the first meeting was to be held at nine o'clock, I was sitting at breakfast when I began to get an entire sequence of thoughts, which, I realized, was the agenda I needed for the meeting. As a consequence, the meeting flowed smoothly and the project was off to a good start. When nothing like this occurred before the next meeting, I simply listened to what the other members had to say. I became aware, as I listened, that I had overlooked an important step in the procedure. Although the next meeting was a month away, I began to worry that I might forget something else, if I failed to give more thought to the project. Two or three nights later, I awoke at 3:00 A.M. with an insight of what I needed to remember for the next meeting; I got up and wrote this down, then went back to bed. Soon, a similar reminder came and I again got up and began writing. When this happened a third time I thought, in exasperation, "Why, at 3:00 A.M.?" I was then too awake to sleep, so, I meditated. Presently I saw moving clouds that, as I watched, formed into a wry smiling face that said, by thought transference, "If you would not have become impatient through doubting, you would have received the help at a more convenient time."

The joy attending the Creative Experience is great. We are not unlike the homely chicken, who upon laying her eggs, clucks loudly to announce her feat. We may want to sing or "let our minds go." The *I Ching* says, however, to keep joy in bounds. If we give way to this feeling, the birthing process halts and the song or feeling of joy takes over. The Creative Experience is like an entire birthing process: first the head comes through, then the shoulders, then the hips and feet, then the afterbirth. We must let the whole thing happen with an attitude of patience, otherwise we receive only a part of the message, and although it is a complete image, we may draw conclusions prematurely about the context in which the image is to be understood. The context has to come through, too, otherwise we have the egg without knowing what to do with it. Our presumptuous ego takes over and makes of it what it

129

will, for its own purposes. I have often had three-part meditations, any part of which might have been mistaken for a single message if I had jumped to that conclusion. The Creative has a way of signalling when the meditation or insight is complete. It is as if something says, "That is all." Sometimes we understand it to be: "That is all for now; more will come later, as you need it." The painter who ignores this feeling inside himself ruins his work by intellectually deciding to add or subtract from the painting, and the inventor creates needless problems for himself if he fails to let go of matters at this point; everything he does will have to be undone if he is to re-discover the direction in which the Creative is to take him.

The Creative Experience comes on its own terms. It is a gift from the source of all wisdom. As it is put in *Grace* (22), it is "a white horse" that "comes as if on wings." The winged horse "is the symbol of the thoughts that transcend all limits of space and time." We may use the knowledge gained in this way, but not possess or misuse it. If we do misuse it, we find that a penalty is attached. All that is necessary is that we sincerely seek and humbly receive. Through retaining our humility and conscientiousness, we turn these gifts into a way of life that will guide and aid those around us. Then our joy is great; it is not that of the excitement that is experienced on first coming into contact with the Creative, but that of fulfillment and completion, of harmony and oneness with all things. Nothing is so great as the serenity and appreciation one feels in seeing the Creative Hand in everything.

7.
GOALS

The *I Ching* mentions "goals" in several hexagrams and lines. *Fellowship with Men* (13) says that "true fellowship among men must be based upon a concern that is universal. It is not the private interests of the individual that create lasting fellowship among men, but rather the goals of humanity. That is why it is said that fellowship with men in the open succeeds. If unity of this kind prevails, even difficult and dangerous tasks...can be accomplished." Indeed, the very name of this hexagram implies that fellowship and unity are among the great goals of mankind. Other hexagrams which concern the universal goals are *Peace* (11) and *Gathering Together* (45). The fourth line of *Gathering Together* speaks of a person who seeks to gather people together: "Since he is not striving for any special advantages for himself but is working unselfishly to bring about general unity, his work is crowned with success." Similarly, the third line of *Before Completion* (64) urges us not to "lose sight of the goal."

While in the above lines the *I Ching* counsels us not to doubt our goals to rectify relationships and to achieve peace and unity between people, it does not want us to become goal-oriented. In the second line of *Innocence* (25) we are counseled not to "count on the harvest while plowing." From the viewpoint of the *I Ching*, the great goals of mankind are achieved only through each of us following our own path. If we look at the goal in terms of wanting it to materialize, our perseverance will be undermined. To achieve our goals we need to keep them in mind without fastening our inner eye upon them. They will materialize only as a result of our keeping on the path of innocence, docility and acceptance. Keeping on the path, therefore, becomes our goal. As the second line in *The Receptive* (2) says, "Straight, square, great, without purpose, yet nothing remains unfurthered."

This is not to say we should not contemplate and recognize the universal goals of mankind, or our personal goals. Such recognition is necessary, and holding to the idea that they are worthwhile and attainable is part of following our path.

Universal Goals

The greater goals of mankind are those of equality, justice, peace, and human-heartedness; they involve the ascendancy of the superior man over the inferior man in such a way that factions between people, brought on by indulgence in petty likes and dislikes, disappear. Man is at one with himself and with nature. There is no longer any opposition between the human will and the Divine Will.

In contemplating the call made in *Fellowship with Men* (13) to free ourselves of those reservations of attitude by which we set ourselves apart as special, we recognize some decadent social attitudes which are "spoiled" from the *I Ching* point of view. For instance, the view that man was given dominion over the earth and all things in a proprietorial way, gives him the idea that he is special and has the right to do so as he will with what he possesses. The hexagram *Possession in Great Measure* (14) counsels a different view toward possessions: "A magnanimous, liberal-minded man should not regard what he possesses as his exclusive personal property, but should place it at the disposal of the ruler or of the people at large. In so doing he takes the right attitude toward his possession, which as private property can never endure." The ruler, in this case, is the Sage, or what is good, generally. Nor does the superior man sacrifice his higher nature for considerations of vanity or the pleasures of the senses. The top line of *Preponderance of the Great* (28) says, "There are things that are more important than life." From the cosmic point of view, all things have dignity and are worthy of respect. To force-feed ducks and geese for the benefit of our sense of taste is to sacrifice the higher aspects of the soul to the benefit of the lower aspects. The superior man keeps himself correct and never assumes the right to be insensitive to suffering.

Suffering, perhaps, cannot be eliminated. Once I had a meditation experience in response to remembering an old Russian friend who had lived through the Bolshevist Revolution. He had said he could not believe there was a God, for if there was, how could such a God permit the suffering he had seen, to happen? In the meditation I saw the face of an older man. His expression exhibited what I can only describe as "all the suffering in the world." It was as if he had witnessed every terrible thing that had ever happened, and his expression was that of a deep commiseration. Immediately I realized that it was the face of the Sage in yet one more guise, and the message of this face was that the Creative can only work through us. Misery and suffering exist because we fail to do our small part. We are not expected to do it all, but everything that we do about correcting ourselves alleviates just that much suffering.

It is not that a permanent and ideal state of peace is ever achieved, for in the Tao of things, increase, or a harmonious balance between things, is always followed by decrease, or imbalance, and decrease changes back once again to increase. Change is the Tao of existence. But if we do not take up the space needed by others, and if our requirements are reasonable and just, there is space and enough for all living things. Just as through the creative effort of those who care, the long-term trajectory of progress upwards towards peace is made possible in the world, a long term trajectory downwards occurs because people relax into luxurious and decadent habits of mind.

The hexagram *Peace* (11) envisions the world, and society in general, being brought to a state of order and harmony. The ruler (Sage) furthers the people, and the people, by their ordering activity, further nature. "This controlling and furthering activity of man in his relation to nature is the work on nature that rewards him." Man, in harmony with himself, his human fellows, and nature, brings an end to all feuds. The light principle is in the key position—the "good elements of society occupy a central position and are in control....the spirit of heaven rules in man."

Gathering Together (45) presents an image of people rallying behind what is correct in the community through their "collective piety." "Only collective moral force can unite the world." This is made possible through "great offerings," meaning the voluntary sacrifice of personal ends wherever they conflict with the great and good ends of society

133

and nature.

Holding Together (8) also lists some of the essential components by which people may be brought together into a correctly functioning social order. Human society should "hold together through a community of interests that allows each individual to feel himself a member of a whole. The central power of a social organization must see to it that every member finds that his true interest lies in holding together with it." There must be a "real rallying point." The very purpose for social organization is "that all may complement and aid one another through holding together." "Police measures are not necessary." The people "cleave to their ruler of their own volition. The same principle of freedom is valid for life in general." Indeed, throughout the *I Ching* the principle of freedom to follow and to choose echo over and over. The only bonds are those created by natural affection; the only leadership is that created by inner truth, combined with gentleness and friendliness. *The Joyous* says in this regard that when "the hearts of men are won by friendliness, they are led to take all hardships upon themselves willingly, and if need be will not shun death itself, so great is the power of joy over men." Force, pressure, even the mildest use of leverage is against the dignity of the individual. Such an ordering requires a social organization by which "outer rank corresponds with inner worth," and the leaders hold those around them purely by the power and truth of their personalities. As the *judgment* in *Following* (17) says, it is only when our leaders are consistent in "doing right" together with "no blame" that we can follow them without coming to harm.

Individual Goals

Although our original aim on consulting the *I Ching* may be to rescue ourselves from the grip of difficulties, to achieve this goal we find that we are required to rescue the others with whom we are involved. Gaining help from the Sage gives us this cosmic obligation. In the hexagram *Difficulty at the Beginning* (3), our obligation to rescue the others is pictured as a wagon that we (as the horse) must pull. When we seek to rid ourselves of this burden, we get the line, "Horse and wagon part. Strive for union," and the explanation, "It is our duty to act, but we lack sufficient power. However, an opportunity to make connections offers itself. It must be seized. Neither false pride nor false reserve should deter us. Bringing oneself to take the first step, even when it involves a certain degree of self-abnegation, is a sign of inner clarity." We invariably receive this line when we are tempted to give up on others. In whatever ways our relationships have failed due to faulty attitudes on our part, we must correct these attitudes. This obligation to rescue others is not performed as we might think—with our watching their path and interfering in their lives; doing the right thing may isolate us from them if rectification calls for going on our way alone; if that is the only way an eventual unity may be achieved, it is necessary to go in that direction. Holding to the potential for good within others may be our primary goal during much of our self-development.

Through correcting ourselves we strengthen the family. In the framework of family ties, the "performance of moral duty is made easy through natural affection," and this practice of correct behavior can then be "widened to include human relationships in general," as *The Family* (37) explains. The family is the basic unit of society—indeed, it is society in microcosm; if we break the chain of decadent social attitudes that are passed from one generation to another through the family, the social order may be renewed. As *Work on What Has Been Spoiled* (18) points out, decadent traditions are carried on partly because they are our only example, and partly because we need to justify our parents to ourselves. When, as fathers and mothers, we settle our problems rather than give up on each other, we maintain a tradition of patience and perseverance in the way we relate to people. If, on the other hand, we are impatient and vindictive, our children will adopt these attitudes and they will be passed out into society through the way they relate to others.

The common view of Chinese philosophy—that if we would change the world we must first correct the state, and that if we would correct the state, we must first correct the community, and that if we would correct the community we must first correct the family, and that if we correct the family, we must first correct the individual—undoubtedly comes

135

from the *I Ching*, which holds the view that a real and enduring influence always proceeds from within outwards.

Apart from the obvious ethical benefits of following our
path, a higher purpose is written into the lines and hexagrams
of the *I Ching*. Rescuing ourselves and others from the difficulties of external life is preparatory to fulfilling the highest
meaning of our lives.

A Job To Do

Anyone who chooses to develop himself finds that his
path leads to an important job. In following our Tao and
completing our spiritual journey, we are part of the great
spiritual evolution of the universe. Not everyone answers the
call to develop himself spiritually. The fifth line of *Holding
Together* (8) points out that whether we follow this path is
entirely up to us. "There is depicted here a ruler, or influential man, to whom people are attracted. Those who come to
him he accepts, those who do not come are allowed to go on
their own way. He invites none, flatters none—all come of
their own free will."

Certainly, the path is rigorous. The training requires a
certain withdrawal from normal life—a withdrawal that frequently separates us from old friends and family members,
for a time. Meanwhile, we gain the companionship of the
Sage, and find others who become companions of the
journey. Our withdrawal is not planned, it simply happens.
Nor is it a complete withdrawal, as in going to a monastery;
we usually have to go on with the business of life, earning a
living or raising a family, while we work with the Sage in the
daily classroom of experience. It may be all we can do to
maintain these essential activities; extra activities require
more energy than we have available.

Many lines in the hexagrams discuss this withdrawal. If
we are meditating, we often see our inner world location as
being isolated from everyone but the Sage. The fifth line in
Fellowship with Men (13) speaks of our sense of loneliness:
"Men bound in fellowship first weep and lament, but afterward they laugh. After great struggles they succeed in
meeting." This line confirms our eventual reunification with
those with whom we have deep and unbreakable inner connections.

The work that is achieved through withdrawal is described in the sixth line of *Work on What Has Been Spoiled* (18): "He does not serve kings and princes, sets himself higher goals." Withdrawal, it cautions, "does not imply a right to remain idle or sit back and merely criticize. Such withdrawal is justified only when we strive to realize in ourselves the higher aims of mankind. For although the Sage remains distant from the turmoil of life, he creates incomparable human values for the future."

This work requires time, for every lesson in self-development has to be directly experienced, and every fear unmasked. Through encountering numerous dead-ends and making our way through the maze of beliefs and disbeliefs, inner truth accumulates to a strength we never had before. Our inner development has been like that of a seed that sprouted and worked its way through the soil to reach the air and light, then to slowly grow to become a tree—well-developed and firmly rooted. Such an image is given in the hexagram *Development* (53).

The effect of character purification is like that of producing electricity; electricity is generated by rotating a solid piece of pure copper inside windings of pure copper wire; this causes electrical charges to be given off onto wires as electrical current. This is possible because, in pure copper, all the molecules line up in exactly the same way. When our will is aligned with the Cosmic Will and our inner mind and heart are purified, the same powerful effect occurs.

In responding to the *I Ching's* call to purification, we sacrifice all ego-aspects of our personality as impurities. In *The Ting* (50), a call is made to sacrifice the "highest earthly value," which, when we think about it, is the right to lead ourselves—as our ego puts it. This step to self-purification is perhaps the most difficult to make, but it is the one that creates true inner power. The purity of spirit that creates inner power is equivalent to a complete absence of mistrust in our relationship with the Sage and Fate. This purity expresses itself as modesty and acceptance, and as mildness and steadfastness. In practical terms, it means allowing ourselves to be led blindly and joyfully by the Sage, and by letting what Fate puts before us to happen without resistance from us.

Enlightenment progresses in levels. One plateau succeeds

another as the spiritual baby in us matures and we attain the cosmological view. It is easier to see with clarity, and clarity of mind is retained for longer periods. We become more wary of the encroachment of indolence and carelessness, consequently the problems that vexed us severely at first do not trouble us now. We are up to the challenges, partly because we know our limits, and partly because we know when we need to ask for help.

Enlightenment means, literally, lifting off the overburden. Virtually the first half of our life is spent accumulating an overburden of half-truths and outright falsehoods that we have accepted both unthinkingly and thinkingly. These have accumulated into a belief-system which results in self-conflict and disharmony with others. In undoing this overburden we rid ourselves of weights we have carried for years without realizing their deteriorating and exhausting effects, until we are liberated from them.

Three conceptions in particular found most of our spiritual problems. They tend to be expressed as disbeliefs. The first is that we are born evil. The second is our disbelief in the fundamental goodness of life, so that we doubt that by being simple, serene, and sincere, life will work out for us. The third is our disbelief in God as an active presence and force for good in the world. Thus we limit God—the God that is around us in the grandeur of everything that exists, and in every expression of the sublime. Most of all, we slander God by creating him in the image of our inferior man—as selfish, egotistical, unapproachable, uncaring, immodest, jealous, vindictive, and prone to capricious moods and destructive temper tantrums. Thus we lose sight of the fact that God is totally good, totally beautiful, and present in everything—the living and the dying, the flowing out and flowing in of God. In coming into harmony with ourselves we feel the true nature and presence of God, and the immediacy of God. In being sincere and following the good, we attain the powerful help and come to know the caring of God. In coming to know the Sage, we feel the friendship and sense of humor that is also God.

Growth through the successive stages of enlightenment cultivates three main virtues: *Simplicity, Sincerity,* and *Serenity.*

Simplicity is mentioned in the first line of *Treading* (10) as the ability to work in a certain way: to do what is good for its own sake. "When a man is dissatisfied with modest circumstances, he is restless and ambitious and tries to advance, not for the sake of accomplishing anything worthwhile, but merely in order to escape from lowliness and poverty....Once his purpose is achieved, he is certain to become arrogant and luxury-loving....On the other hand, a man who is good at his work is content to behave simply. He wishes to make progress in order to accomplish something. When he attains his goal, he does something worthwhile, and all is well."

Sincerity is to answer the moment as it presents itself; if we don't know the answer, it doesn't mean we leave the field to the enemy; it means we wait, clinging docilely to the power of the Creative. If the answer still doesn't come, we wait, avoiding conflict. Sometimes it is necessary to say what we believe, modestly, so as not to assent to what is wrong, but if we take hold of issues or press forward with our views so as to make an impression, or if we defend ourselves in the ambition to improve the situation, we go too far. In all cases, sincerity is to listen to the inner voice that arises from serenity and detachment.

Serenity refers to an acceptance of events which comes, not from defeat, but from the courage to meet all things, good and bad, with equanimity. It is a confidence to let things be and to let them become. It is to listen to our inner voice and really act upon it. It is the ability to accept limits, accept duty, accept predicaments, accept accidents, accept adversity, accept good times. This acceptance is not that of the beginning swimmer who, on finding his feet off the bottom, allows himself to drown, but of one who, somehow, begins to swim. This is a sort of confidence that can be attained only through growth and enlightenment, for it is founded on a firm inner realization of the hidden forces that control life.

Armed with these three treasures—Simplicity, Sincerity, and Serenity, each person finds a sphere in which to work. In this sphere he does not merely fraternize with those who, like himself, are on the path, but "mingles freely with all sorts of people, friends or foes. That is the only way to achieve something," we are informed in the first line of *Following* (17). The line further counsels that we must "have firm principles," so that we do not "vacillate where there is only a question of current opinion." As Lao Tzu put it, "bad men are the charge of good men," remarking that "not to cherish one's charge is to be on the wrong road." If we consider it, the world is made evil by good people abandoning and factionalizing themselves against "bad people." As the Sage humbles himself to help us, through sacrificing anger and our sense of rights, we humble ourselves to help others. This produces "increase" which "alone has power to help the world."

We begin to see that all of us who are cleaning up the small areas of our life are like tent-poles holding up a big tent. It is in this way that the Sage forms his invisible kingdom. We are given the image, in many lines and hexagrams, of a kingdom run by a wise and able ruler. We become extensions of his rule as "officials in the provinces." The very structure of the hexagram symbolizes a kingdom. The second line represents the position of the official in the provinces, while the third line represents that of the "minister" and the fifth of the "ruler" or prince. The sixth line represents the Sage who is outside the affairs of men, but who makes his decrees felt from the cloud heights.

"An enlightened ruler and an obedient servant—this is the condition on which great progress depends," says a line from *Progress* (35). The second line of *Obstruction* (39) says, "The king's servant is beset with obstruction upon obstruction, but it is not his fault." The third line of *Increase* (42) says, "It is important that there should be men who mediate between leaders and followers." The fourth line in *Gathering Together* (45) describes a man "who gathers people around him in the name of the ruler"; as a consequence, everything he does succeeds. In *Approach* (19) we are warned, as servants of the ruler, to avoid the dangers of power and influence and to remember the higher person who sponsors us. In the top line of *Nourishment* (27), we are reminded of our heavy responsibility to nourish others correctly. In *Modesty* (15) we are cautioned to be modest in spite of our merit, and not be officials who decline to fulfill their responsibility.

As servants and officials in this hidden kingdom, we earn recognition and win help to accomplish our tasks. In *The Taming Power of the Great* (26), we are honored by the ruler for adhering to our principles. In *Progress* (35), we are informed that the leader who does not abuse his great influence, but who uses it instead for the benefit of the ruler, is showered with presents from the great man, who "invites him continually to his court." In *Following* (17) it is said, "the King introduces him to the Western Mountain," which symbolizes how well-pleased the ruler is in his servant. In *Pushing Upward* (46), the "King offers him Mount Ch'i," which is still another award. In *Increase* (42), through sacrificing self-interest to help others, the follower is "presented before God" by the ruler. In *The Army* (7), by achieving victory in the "wars" we are awarded "realms."

Thus we wear the invisible mantles given us by the Sage. The second line of *The Army* points out that our decorations are earned. Although each of us on the path knows the other and there is true comradeship, the kingdom always remains invisible and unorganized. No person can grant us our spiritual decorations, nor can any take them away. There is nothing to cling to such as an organization, but we are satisfied. We are unapproved and unofficial, but it doesn't matter. We find our approval and our officialdom conferred upon us by the stars. Nor is everyone who is on the path a user of the *I Ching*. As Lao Tzu said, a great many people who never heard of the Tao have followed it their whole lives.

The way of Tao is to remain hidden. The way of the Sage is to remain unnoticed. The wisest thing is often hidden in the simplest event. Lao Tzu said, "Fools laugh at the Tao. If they did not laugh at it, it would not be the Tao." How else can it be that throwing pennies can teach one to be wise? It is the way of Tao to rear wise people in uncommon ways.

Although we don't see the Sage, we begin to perceive his hand in everything. Lao Tzu said, he is "the mother of the world" in one line, and in another, he is "the father of the world." What we come to value are the hidden things; we know and accept that they must be hidden and that they will never be approved by a consensus of opinion.

We are able to keep our positions in this invisible kingdom as long as we remain "wanderers" in a strange land. If we feel secure, we begin to presume; if we presume, we lose the way. We retain our positions only so long as we continue conscientiously and sincerely on our paths. No one is so well-established that he may not err. "The highest good," we are informed in *Contemplation* (20), is not being free of blame, but in "knowing how to become free of blame."

Book II of the *I Ching* says, "He who succeeds in endowing his work with this regenerative power creates something organic, and...enduring." Again, "the perfected nature of man, sustaining itself and enduring, is the gateway of Tao and justice." And again, "The *Book of Changes* imparts divine mystery to the nature and action of the person who puts his trust in it; thus he meets every event correctly and aids the Gods in governing the world." "In knowing the Tao of change and transformation, such a person knows the action of the Gods. Such a person attains the divine forces, and accomplishes change and order by divine means. The instrument of his perfection is the *Book of Changes.*" In my own work with the *I Ching* I have found it to be no less than all these things, realized long ago by the ancients who travelled the road before us.

Our job is no less than to put the world in order. We can do this only by being responsive to the Divine Will. The ability of man to act as a conduit for the Divine Will makes him the third primal power, giving him a unique capacity and responsibility to "further." As the top line of *Standstill* (12) says, "left to itself," everything changes toward "stagnation and disintegration. The time of disintegration...does not change back automatically to a condition of peace and prosperity; effort must be put forth to end it. This shows the creative attitude that man must take if the world is to be put in order." This creative work falls to each person who sees that the job must be undertaken, and who cannot turn his back upon the task.

Index

143

Index

KEEPING STILL (52), 12,20,44,
95-101; 114; activity, 51-87;
concept, 95; method, 95-101
Ken, 19,20,22
key to hexagrams, using the, 24
kindness, 32
King, 141; kingdom, 140,141
knowledge of the heart, 83
Korea, 1
K'un, 19,21
Lao Tzu, 2,12,14,17,36,70,73,
75,83,120,140,141
Leaning Tower of Pisa, 81
lesson plan, 65
Li, 16,19,21
light power or force, 38,47
LIMITATION (60), 67,91,108;
concept, 109,114,138
LITTLE LORD FAUNTLEROY,
Francis Hodgson Burnett, 120
lizard, 3
logic, 79,113
looking ahead, 34,80, 81-84;
aside, 34,80, 81-84, 106;
behind, 34,80, 84-86; as
watching, 109
Lord of Darkness, 50
luck, 59,83
magnificence, 72,84,85
MARRYING MAIDEN, THE (54),
71,104
masculine principle, 17
master (guru), 74
'mean, the', 60,86,114
measuring activity of inferiors,
83,109
meditation, 48,51,96,97-101,
118,127,128; experiences in,
48,74,97,100,118,122,126,
129,133
minister, 40
mirror effect, 74,114,115
'misfortune', 29
misunderstanding as prelude to

understanding, 58,59,81
MODESTY (15), 14,33,140;
quality, 14,56,60,64, 83-85,
89,102,107, 115-121, 127,137
moon, 3,124
mythology, 100,101
natural responses, 35,88,102
no-mind, 128
non-action, 109
North Star, 12
NOURISHMENT (27), 81,94,96,
140; concept, 94,95,140
numbers, 18,22,23
OBSTRUCTION (39), 140; concept, 52,53
officials in the provinces, 140
oneness, 31,44,122,130
OPPOSITION (38), 59
OPPRESSION (47), 76,90
order, 15,16,28,30,88,102,133,
134,142
original nature, 32,34,44
ORPHEUS AND EURIDICE, 101
pacts, 34,41,43,51,80
passion, 46
path, 83, 102-104, 109,110,120,
136,141
patience, 39,40,57,102,113
pause in progress, 73,127
PEACE (11), 21,131,133;
concept, 133
penalty, 130
penetration as a principle, 111
pennies, 22,66
perseverance, 57,81,87,102,107,
109,111
personality, preservation of, 117
pig, 42
pity, 73
POSSESSION IN GREAT
MEASURE (14), 85,106,132
possessions, 132
POWER OF THE GREAT, THE,
(34), 42